Against Storytelling

Literary Activism

Series Editor: Amit Chaudhuri

Against Storytelling

―――――――

Edited by
Amit Chaudhuri

  CENTRE FOR
**The Creative and
The Critical**

Published by Westland Books, a division of Nasadiya Technologies Private Limited, in 2024

No. 269/2B, First Floor, 'Irai Arul', Vimalraj Street, Nethaji Nagar, Alapakkam Main Road, Maduravoyal, Chennai 600095

Westland and the Westland logo are the trademarks of Nasadiya Technologies Private Limited, or its affiliates.

Anthology copyright © Centre for The Creative and The Critical, Ashoka University, 2024

The copyright for the individual essays vests with the individual authors.

ISBN: 9789360450533

10 9 8 7 6 5 4 3 2 1

The views and opinions expressed in this work are the authors' own and the facts are as reported by them, and the publisher is in no way liable for the same.

All rights reserved

Typeset by Jojy Philip, New Delhi

Printed at Parksons Graphics Pvt. Ltd

No part of this book may be reproduced, or stored in a retrieval system, or transmitted in any form or by any means, electronic, mechanical, photocopying, recording, or otherwise, without express written permission of the publisher.

Contents

A Note on the Series	vii
Against Storytelling: Mission Statement	xi
Lyric Embarrassment: Or, Why I Can't tell a Story *Tiffany Atkinson*	1
Storytelling and Forgetfulness *Amit Chaudhuri*	18
Journalism and the Triumph of the Story *Jeremy Harding*	32
UP Against Storytelling, for David Antin *Charles Bernstein*	43
'What Difference Does It Make?': For and Against Storytelling via the Novels of Kiran Nagarkar *Anjum Hasan*	76
I Don't Have Wings: Vinod Kumar Shukla *Arvind Krishna Mehrotra*	87
A Story in Memory of John Ashbery *Geoffrey O'Brien*	97
Fabricating Texts for Theatre from a Tribal Village in Bengal *Jean-Frédéric Chevallier*	107
Beyond the Tangible *Gurvinder Singh*	137
Notes on the Contributors	143

A Note on the Series

'Literary activism' is a project that began in 2014 with a series of annual symposia. Its aim was to create a space for the kind of discussion on creativity no longer available in mainstream contexts (literary festivals, book launches) or in academic ones (conferences, classrooms, monographs). The literary activism website—https//www. literaryactivism.com—was created in 2020, and the Centre for the Creative and the Critical at Ashoka University came into existence in 2022 at Ashoka University to give this project a home, and to look at the kind of thinking that writing and the arts comprise.

This new imprint, 'literary activism', is meant to carry forward these ambitions in the realm of publishing. The art vs science debate is now a historical relic, but what interests us is the possibility of creating a meaning for writing that's separate from market value and academic legitimacy. And we wish to recall that art and writing are not synonymous with the generalised academic discipline called the 'humanities': they have an angularity to it, and to the social science perspectives the humanities are now subsumed under. The 'literary activism' imprint wishes not only to publish good writing, but to pursue this angularity.

What follows are papers that were presented on 23–24 February 2018 at the India International Centre, New Delhi on the occasion of the fourth symposium ('Against Storytelling') in the Literary Activism series of symposia, hosted that year jointly by Ashoka University and the University of East Anglia. The papers/essays were a response to the mission statement which had been sent to participants along with the invitation. Only one essay, Jeremy Harding's, is from 15 March 2019, when a one-day offshoot of the symposium was repeated at Columbia University's Institute for Ideas and Imagination, Paris.

Against Storytelling: Mission Statement

About a decade ago, I interrupted a talk I was giving to a small group of international writers and academics gathered in Delhi to say, 'Fuck storytelling.'

My respondent, a British Asian literary journalist, later said, while commenting on my talk, how 'shocked' she'd been by my remark. It wasn't the expletive she objected to, but my attack on 'storytelling', which had been so 'empowering to peoples and cultures.' 'Storytelling' had, by now, become a sacred cow that you insulted at your own risk.

My reasons for making that remark were at least twofold. The first had to do with the fact that—given we live in an ethos in which the event is of primary significance, and whatever is significant has to be construed as an event of some sort—it follows that part of the reason stories are important is because they contain a happening, or happenings, in a character's or a place's life. It also follows that the eventless can't be the proper subject of a story.

My second reason has to do with my discomfiture with the idea that 'storytelling' is a feature of non-Western culture, and a valuable resource, as a result, of a postcolonial politics that sets itself up against the Enlightenment. A glance at non-Western artistic expression reveals, however, a deep commitment to forms outside of what we now think of as 'narrative' (synecdoche, for instance, and other means of poetic elision).

In an essay I wrote more than a decade ago, 'Notes on the Novel after Globalisation', I'd remarked that globalisation, by the turn of the millennium, had become a kind of narrative—a lateral, interconnected network from which there was no escape, and from which no one evidently desired to escape—and this privileging of *a narrative that had no 'outside'* (globalisation) led to the marginalisation of the poetic, to the genre of the novel becoming synonymous with the 'mainstream', and to a particular celebration of narrative. Let me quote a section from the essay:

> Another co-ordinate that should be mentioned in this mapping of narrativity as a crucial critical and political conceit is the idea of 'storytelling'. It's a notion that didn't really exist in any persuasive way on the intellectual landscape thirty years ago. Its rise is related to the fashioning of the discourse of postcoloniality; 'storytelling', with its kitschy magic and its associations of postcolonial empowerment, is seen to emanate from the immemorial funds of orality in the non-Western world, and might be interpreted as a critique of the inscribed word, and its embeddedness in Western forms of knowledge. 'Storytelling', then, is also an alternative to disciplines like history in the Western humanities; if it is now an ingredient in history-writing, it is so precisely to mark a break with the Eurocentric, the literate, the elite. No wonder that the notion is invoked almost always with an air of glamour and celebration. Both the concordances and the distinctions between this invocation and Walter Benjamin's recovery of the figure of 'the storyteller' are instructive; for Benjamin was by no means an unequivocal advocate of narrativity. Thus, in the first paragraph of 'The Task of the Translator': 'No poem is intended for the reader, no picture for the beholder, no symphony for the listener.' Benjamin is expressing the profound modernist desire for disjunction, a breach in the lateral weave of the fabric; it's an image strikingly different from the one of simultaneous readership that comprises Anderson's nationhood. Today, in the early twenty-first century, we've entered yet another cultural and political phase, after the shifts and reappraisals represented, in their time, by modernity and post-modernity. This shift asks us to look at narrative once again; and it asks the novelist to be careful about the point at which 'storytelling' begins to collude with the narrativity of globalisation.

The symposium in February 2018 aims to discuss questions raised by the sacredness we attribute to this apparently timeless act of recounting and telling.

Amit Chaudhuri
June 2017

Lyric Embarrassment: Or, Why I Can't Tell a Story

Tiffany Atkinson

When I first received Amit's concept note for the symposium with its opening provocation, 'Fuck storytelling!' I felt a little pop of relief in my chest, and in the parts of me that I think love poetry and theoretical writing more than narrative writing, and I thought, 'Yes, I agree, fuck it, fuck storytelling.' How great to have a chance to think about writing without having to address that demand first and foremost, because it's one that I find increasingly both exhausting and predictable. Don't get me wrong, I do enjoy stories, I love hearing them and I love reading them, but I don't write them and I don't really think in them. I don't think I am a born storyteller, so I find myself resisting first of all the association of all models of literacy with storytelling, and also the demand to couch everything in terms of story, from one's own personal life to—in the university world, for example—research 'trajectories' and learning 'outcomes' and so forth.

Nonetheless, I can see, obviously, the value and merit in storytelling, so my take against storytelling here is not really so much antagonism or direct opposition, or a desire to overthrow (which I suppose is in itself an agonistic narrative structure), but more a kind of leaning against, an askance-ness, a benign friction or pressure that at least tries to assert the value of alternative notions of language-use. The idea of a *benign friction* is something that interests me at the moment because it's how I would describe embarrassment, and recently I've been trying to follow through a hunch that more than any other literary genre, poetry is a field prickly with embarrassment, despite the best efforts of literary theory or creative writing teaching (which are aspects of my day job) to behave otherwise. This may just be making virtue of necessity since poetry has always felt like the embarrassing other of my critical work, and the predicament of actually being a poet can be just embarrassing all round.

For example, in his polemic, *The Hatred of Poetry* (2016), poet and critic Ben Lerner describes an awkward encounter with his dentist when the subject of his own profession comes up. He reflects, 'There's embarrassment for the poet—couldn't you get a real job and put your childish ways behind you?—but there's also embarrassment on the part of the non-poet because having to acknowledge one's total alienation from poetry chafes against the early association of poem and self.' He continues, 'I had the sensation that Dr X, as he knocked the little mirror against my molars, was contemptuous of the idea that genuine poetry could issue from such an opening.'

I will return to the dentist's surgery, and to the question of what may issue from such an opening, in due course. But I think that most poets would recognise the tenor of Lerner's encounter and indeed I would supplement his observation with one of my own: the follow-up question that is very often asked when I admit to writing poetry, which is, 'Oh! But have you ever thought about writing a novel?' and there's an unspoken but palpable second clause to that, which is, '… when you grow up.' And closer to home, my father, when he read my recent collection (I don't come from a literary family at all) said, 'Oh—what poets should do [effectively to put readers like him out of their misery] is to have the poems on one page, and then on the other page a couple of paragraphs by someone telling us what the poem was really about. Why,' he wondered, 'hadn't my publisher thought of this?'

So, in response to the palpable flinch that I think poetry seems to provoke in others and sometimes in oneself as a poet, I've been trying out this kind of *what if* question: that is, what if we turn towards the embarrassments of poetry reading, writing, and teaching, perhaps in an effort to find them fruitful? This follows a mode of thinking that feels to me more like the *writing* of a poem, which can be uncomfortable and more about hunches and the turning up of carpets, than the tidy literary housekeeping of criticism. It is composition by discomposure perhaps. In this essay, I'd like to try to think through some aspects of lyric embarrassment as a kind of resistance to story and to storytelling, both for the writer and reader of poetry, and hopefully to argue that there may be something to be gained from this. But first, I'd like to draw out some of the connections between embarrassment and lyric poetry.

With the exception of Christopher Ricks's *Keats and Embarrassment* of 1974, embarrassment has received short shrift in literary studies, despite the recent 'affective turn' in literary criticism. Shame, on the other hand, is the subject of a growing body of critical work, for example, Elspeth Probyn's *Blush: Faces of Shame* from 2005, and an edited collection called *Shame and Modern Writing*, published by Routledge in 2018. In poetry, there have also been a number of publications that have to do specifically with shame—for example, Nuar Alsadir and Denise Riley have both written powerfully about lyric shame. But I'm interested in how easily discussions of embarrassment quickly shift into a higher-octane, higher-status affective language of guilt, shame, dislike or hatred (to use Ben Lerner's example). This seems to be part of a general slippage from a kind of low-stakes affect to high-stakes (or more reliably narrative or melodramatic) affect. Shame tells a better story than embarrassment. Ben Lerner's book, for example, begins with a couple of interesting anecdotes about embarrassment, but since his theme is hatred, the rhetoric of the book quickly undergoes a compelling but rather grandiose affective inflation composed around the tragic slippage between our expectations of poetry in the abstract and the falling short of actual poems. Thus, he writes, 'You'll move to write a poem, you feel called upon to sing, because of that transcendent impulse. But as soon as you move from that impulse to the actual poem, the song of the infinite is compromised by the finitude of its terms. Thus the poet is a tragic figure, the poem is always a record of failure.' I don't want to dismiss this argument—though it's possible that what Lerner describes is the condition of language *per se*, which is not particular to poetry and something we all have to contend with—but I would like to arrest its possibly rather masculine hurry towards modernist, Romantic or indeed Platonic stories of the hobbled sublime, in order to dwell itchily on its initial, softer premise of embarrassment. This is comic more than tragic, absurd more than sublime, miniaturist more than epic, gauche more than urbane, a frisson more than a dialectical position, a niggle more than an epiphany; in other words, not very promising narrative material. Nonetheless, it is an affective field that governs an astonishing proportion of everyday behaviour. Sociological theory is pretty unanimous about this, often citing Erving Goffman's influential 1967 essay, 'Embarrassment and Social Organization' to the effect that 'the social codes which permit daily interaction would lose their force without the threat or possibility of embarrassment', and that, 'a quiet but compelling drive to avoid embarrassment pervades our daily life'.

Be that as it may, I'd like you, just as a brief experiment, to summon a recent embarrassment of your own, and consider how hard it is to dwell in that affective moment. Embarrassment is volatile and unstable, and very quickly peels off in another direction, generally either becoming comic and something to laugh or shrug off—a nonverbal dismissal that I suppose forestalls actual communication; or in another direction, which I tried to describe earlier, towards something with more moral and narrative gravitas, like shame or mortification; and as with Lerner's flight into hatred, I feel compelled to put my foot in the door that swings between embarrassment and shame, and to uncouple these sister states.

The foot in the door is an apt metaphor as it turns out, not only recalling the feet of metric verse but also summoning the very etymology of embarrassment, a much younger word than shame and having precisely to do with obstruction. Originally meaning to block or impede, its etymology derives from the fifteenth-century Spanish *embarazar* and Portuguese *embaraçar,* a compound of the prefix *em* and *baraço*, meaning a cord; probably a reference to animals being restrained by a cord or a leash. It retains its obstructive meaning until the mid-eighteenth century when it acquires its modern transitive aspect of making a person feel awkward or self-conscious. Two early examples from the *Oxford English Dictionary* are, from 1751, John Cleland's *Memoirs of a Coxcomb*: 'My steadiness of gaze began to embarrass and give her pain', and from 1796, Mary Wollstonecraft's *Letters in Sweden, Norway, and Denmark*: 'I wished to have had a room to myself; for their attention, and rather distressing observation, embarrassed me extremely'.

Shame, by contrast, comes from the Old English *scamu* via the Gothic *skama*, inferring the covering of oneself, and signalling much stronger states of dishonour, ignominy and disgrace, apparently acquiring a transitive turn around the thirteenth century, when it came to imply fear of such dishonour, thus accommodating a switch from masculine codes of dishonour to feminine ones of modesty. For example, from Chaucer's *Wife of Bath's Prologue* (1368): 'In habit, maad with chastitee and shame, Ye wommen shul apparaille yow' (in habits made with chastity, not shame, ye women should be garmented). These comparisons certainly bring into focus the common ground between the two states, in their regulatory function around social norms, and a crucial relation to a witnessing other who may be actual or imagined, but who activates a kind of triangulation whereby the self is made self-conscious by their presence. Both terms come to encompass an uneasy association with feminine self-consciousness, which is perhaps where that slippage occurs, but for my purposes today, I'd maintain that they have very different trajectories, and in the spirit of hunches I'd like to follow these differences through a little.

Shame is ancient; embarrassment, modern. Shame a moral infraction, embarrassment a social one. Shame is essentially religious, embarrassment secular. Shame's relationship to the other is dialectical, a sort of zero-sum game—a contract, a fixing in place of self and other; embarrassment is sticky, infectious and rhizomatic; it is often unclear who the embarrasser and who the embarrassee is (we might recall Lerner's mutually embarrassing encounter with his dentist). Perhaps shame has to do with opposition, embarrassment with contiguity, and where shame asserts boundaries, embarrassment wobbles. Shame potentially activates a redemptive narrative or a symbolic circuitry of retribution, penance, reconciliation; embarrassment seems fundamentally non-narrative, leading nowhere, stranding one hotly in the present, in a peculiar and unscripted intersection of self and other and where one's role in the dynamic is not always entirely clear.

The mutually disconcerting relationship to the other that embarrassment elicits is described by the philosopher Luke Purshouse (2001) in these terms: 'Embarrassment is essentially about the exposure of one person to another. Interpersonal exposure occurs when an aspect of one person, whom I shall term an *exposee*, enters the thoughts and experience of another, the *recipient*. The aspects of the exposee that can be exposed include his physical body, mental states, dispositions of character and actions. Exposure also takes place when one person obtains knowledge about somebody else.' Purshouse also emphasises the reciprocal dynamic of embarrassment, noting that one can be embarrassed when construing oneself as *either* participant in the exposure. There are thus occasions where, he writes, 'It is less clear who is the recipient and who the exposee, and, indeed, where exposure may be a two-way process.'

We might almost call this wobbly condition *reading*, and consider much of our daily lives are governed by *this* benign friction. I'd like to consider how the lyric poem specifically thrives on this wobble, and on how, rather than activating the reparative and narrative moral dimension of shame, it potentially elicits a softer but nonetheless ethical relation to the other or others invoked—or touched—in the reading process. Embarrassment announces a specifically modern relation of contiguity, recognition and contagion, I argue, rather than an ancient and dialectical one of opposition and moral contract. It is moreover, essentially a non-narrative state and as such belongs to the discontinuous instant that is central to lyric poetry. The triangulations of social embarrassment are thus, in many respects, mirrored in the development of the conventions of the modern lyric poem.

The lyric poem of course has a long history, beginning, as its name attests, with song, continuing in written form through the ode and dramatic monologue, all of which own an explicit and coded relationship between the audience and the addressee. But in its generally accepted modern form, the lyric seems to have something of embarrassment embedded in its very structure. I turned to my old undergraduate textbook, M.H. Abrams's *Glossary of Literary Terms* (1956—but still a standard text in the early 1990s) for a hands-on definition, which is, 'any fairly short, non-narrative poem presenting a single speaker who expresses a state of mind or a process of thought and feeling'. The emphasis on reflexive subjectivity as it were 'caught in the act' is clearly a post-Romantic formulation that separates the lyric from the ode in its introverted structure of address, and from the epic and dramatic forms in its construction of the discontinuous lyric instant, divested of wider dramatic or social narrative. Now, already this places the reader in the potentially embarrassing position of an eavesdropper rather than designated audience. John Stuart Mill, in 1833, thus observed that 'eloquence is *heard*, poetry is *overheard* ... Poetry is feeling confessing itself to itself in moments of solitude'. Northrop Frye (1957) later identifies both the artifice of this privacy and its secular nature as enduring features of the modern lyric. He writes, 'The lyric poet normally pretends to be talking to himself or someone else: a spirit of nature, a muse, a personal friend, a lover, a god, a personified abstraction, or a natural object ... The radical of presentation in the lyric is the hypothetical form of what in religion is called the "I-Thou" relationship. The poet, so to speak, turns his back on his listeners.'

I'm really struck by Frye's image of the poet turning his back on his listeners, and how in the context of telling a story, or any utterance for that matter, that would be a very strange physical thing to do. It also occurs to me that the only other time where one tells any kind of story with one's back to the listener is in Freudian psychoanalysis, but alas I haven't time to pursue that thought here! Meanwhile, Barbara Herrnstein Smith (1979) further elucidates the artifice of the lyric as overheard speech when she calls lyric poems 'fictive utterances', as if, she proposes, 'every lyric began with the invisible words, "For example, I (or someone) could say ..."'

The structural embarrassment of the lyric, then, already seems implicit in its status as overheard private utterance, embarrassing for the receiver, yet also an *artificial* and hypothetical utterance which ought to be embarrassing for the poet, whose relationship to the implied speaker of the poem is ambiguous, and at the very least one of pretension. Whether we are writer or reader, the very form of address compromises both of us: the writer, through her simultaneous desire to speak out, but aware of the injunction against pretension; the reader through her audiophilic desire to overhear. The double bind required of the lyric, its desire for the *effect of spontaneous authenticity,* is indeed a conundrum, and the question of register opens further onto a range of hazards around the lyric's supposed relation to 'actual speech'. Too little art may be embarrassing because of its banal claims to profundity (and this is where Ben Lerner's example of William McGonagall's terrible flat-footed metrics—for Lerner an example of a kind of tragic failure of the transcendent impulse—seems to me firmly in the camp of embarrassment, not tragedy). Equally hazardous are the pretentious claims of elevated speech, a residue of the decayed 'I-Thou' relationship described by Northrop Frye. Jonathan Culler (1981) singles out the trope of *apostrophe* as indicative of a specifically lyric cringeworthiness: this is the 'O' that we learn as a characteristic sign of poetic diction, from such immortal lines as 'O Rose, thou art sick!', 'O wild West Wind, thou breath of Autumn's being!', 'Oh! But it is dirty!' etc., but which to the modern reader is the very navel of lyric embarrassment. Culler himself describes apostrophe as 'the pure embodiment of poetic pretension', since the vocative 'O' announces a special *poemy* relationship with its object, while still claiming the status of overheard, spontaneous utterance. Enunciating these exclamations is, of course, awkward all round, at least if the measure of comfort is direct or naturalistic speech. He writes, 'Such apostrophes may complicate or disrupt the circuit of communication, raising questions about who is the addressee, but above all they're embarrassing: embarrassing to me [the reader] and to you [the listener].'

Apostrophes, then, are a block, an embarrassment, bringing about a wobble in the circuit of communication and the storytelling promise that may be suggested by first-person lyric address. But more than that, they are linguistically excessive, and precisely the kind of textual detail that's edited out in the descriptive, summative account of poetry required by practical criticism, or 'unseen appreciation', as I was taught it at school. 'What's Blake really talking about?' Mrs Tucker might have asked class 5B. 'What's *happening* in this line? What do we think that Elizabeth Bishop's trying to say?' He's saying that the rose is sick, Miss. She's telling us the filling station's dirty, Miss. Except that's not it, quite. There is something irreducible about the apostrophe which gets to the very heart of the lyric bind and which is always lost in narrative paraphrase. 'O' describes a specifically lyric circuitry between spontaneous utterance *and* the artifice of poetic language: not either/or, but both at once. But to inhabit that 'O' is as hard as dwelling in embarrassment, the shimmer of affect where one briefly accommodates the flash of multiple exposures—the desire for overheard authenticity and the desire for a special poetic effect—and quite literally doesn't know where to put oneself.

My contention is that there's something valuable in this moment, dramatised by 'O' but actually present in all lyric address, that is lost if it's immediately assimilated into the narrative of shame or sublime linguistic failure, or indeed into more banal narrative paraphrase. The lyric poem is a space where one can momentarily 'touch' the other without shame or mortification, and I say this knowing that in the present climate these are pretty loaded terms. But I mean that there are types of mutual exposure that occur within, as it were, controlled and artificial environments, where one can be momentarily cast adrift in the hypothetical space of 'what it is possible to say', and indeed, 'what it is possible to hear'; where we are positioned neither as innocents nor villains, nor even as ironists, but outside narrative positioning, as recipients (but in our very desire, exposees ourselves) of what it might mean to be human. An embarrassing place, but also one for the genuine, perhaps.

All of which returns me to Ricks's *Keats and Embarrassment* which, taken as a whole, is a valiant effort to dismantle a developmental story of poetic sensibility that privileges 'mature' detachment and irony over the 'naive' and embarrassing effects of enthusiasm, sensory excess and self-disclosure. Let's not forget the mortifying jibes the young Keats received from his peers (Byron, for example, who lambasted 'Johnny Keats's *p-ss a bed* poetry' and described him as always 'f--gg-ing his *Imagination*'). But Ricks reads in Keats's adolescent sensibility a penetrating emotional intelligence, an ethical kind of *embarrassensibility*, if you like. Taking the blush as an example, which like 'O' is a duplicitous signifier, a two-way exposure, at once a sign of modesty and of knowing (and much beloved of Keats), Ricks writes: 'Keats knows the blush of guilt (though even there the recognition of guilt is from one point of view a matter for approbation or at any rate hope—unblushing is always a penetrating accusation and enough to make some people blush). But Keats knows too the blush of innocence … He knows indeed the blush which is made up of both.'

For Ricks, an active dimension of Keats's negative capability, being 'without irritable reaching after fact and reason' is precisely his ability to tolerate embarrassensibility to a degree that destabilises the cliche of Romantic self-governing identity; in Purshouse's terms, to explore the terrain of 'exposure' from as many simultaneous angles as possible. And, of course, the lyric poem is very much tied up with the risks and openness of identity. In Keats's own words, 'A Poet is the most unpoetical thing of anything in existence because he has no Identity.'

I opened with the anecdote of a poet embarrassed at the dentist, and to finish, I'll return to this theme with Elizabeth Bishop's poem 'In the Waiting Room', written in 1967, the same year that Marianne Moore, Bishop's friend and mentor, published the final, stripped-down version of her much-revised poem, 'Poetry'. This fifth revision is the one that Ben Lerner alludes to at the beginning of *The Hatred of Poetry*, and which furnishes him with an embarrassing anecdote about failing to memorise a poem. I'm sure you all know it, but in case not:

> I, too, dislike it.
> Reading it, however, with a perfect contempt for it, one discovers in it, after all, a place for the genuine ('Poetry', Marianne Moore).

So now I will read 'In the Waiting Room', which I'm treating as a sort of sister poem to 'Poetry', and which I was moved to go back to after reading Ben Lerner's anecdote about the dentist.

In the Waiting Room
Elizabeth Bishop, 1967 (1979)

In Worcester, Massachusetts,
I went with Aunt Consuelo
to keep her dentist's appointment
and sat and waited for her
in the dentist's waiting room.
It was winter. It got dark
early. The waiting room
was full of grown-up people,
arctics and overcoats,
lamps and magazines.
My aunt was inside
what seemed like a long time
and while I waited I read
the *National Geographic*
(I could read) and carefully
studied the photographs:
the inside of a volcano,
black, and full of ashes;
then it was spilling over
in rivulets of fire.
Osa and Martin Johnson
dressed in riding breeches,
laced boots, and pith helmets.
A dead man slung on a pole
—'Long Pig', the caption said.
Babies with pointed heads
wound round and round with string;
black, naked women with necks
wound round and round with wire

like the necks of light bulbs.
Their breasts were horrifying.
I read it right straight through.
I was too shy to stop.
And then I looked at the cover:
the yellow margins, the date.
Suddenly, from inside,
came an *oh!* of pain
—Aunt Consuelo's voice—
not very loud or long.
I wasn't at all surprised;
even then I knew she was
a foolish, timid woman.
I might have been embarrassed,
but wasn't. What took me
completely by surprise
was that it was *me*:
my voice, in my mouth.
Without thinking at all
I was my foolish aunt,
I—we—were falling, falling,
our eyes glued to the cover
of the *National Geographic*,
February, 1918.

I said to myself: three days
and you'll be seven years old.
I was saying it to stop
the sensation of falling off
the round, turning world
into cold, blue-black space.
But I felt: you are an *I*,
you are an *Elizabeth*,
you are one of *them*.
Why should you be one, too?
I scarcely dared to look

to see what it was I was.
I gave a sidelong glance
—I couldn't look any higher—
at shadowy gray knees,
trousers and skirts and boots
and different pairs of hands
lying under the lamps.
I knew that nothing stranger
had ever happened, that nothing
stranger could ever happen.

Why should I be my aunt,
or me, or anyone?
What similarities—
boots, hands, the family voice
I felt in my throat, or even
the *National Geographic*
and those awful hanging breasts—
held us all together
or made us all just one?
How—I didn't know any
word for it—how 'unlikely' ...
How had I come to be here,
like them, and overhear
a cry of pain that could have
got loud and worse but hadn't?

The waiting room was bright
and too hot. It was sliding
beneath a big black wave,
another, and another.

Then I was back in it.
The War was on. Outside,
in Worcester, Massachusetts,
were night and slush and cold,

and it was still the fifth
of February, 1918.

If you recall, we left Ben Lerner in the dentist's chair with 'the sensation that Dr X, as he knocked the little mirror against my molars, was contemptuous of the fact that genuine poetry could issue from such an opening'. The matter of what sort of 'genuine' utterance might issue from the open mouth—and the complexity of claiming a voice at all, and for what moreover if not to tell a story—is also central to Bishop's poem which, as well as recounting an embarrassing event, is replete with the dynamics of lyric embarrassment. I'd like to open these out a little, first by confessing a professional embarrassment of my own, which is that when I returned to this poem recently, I realised that I've probably been misreading it all these years, at least according to a certain body of criticism. But because I'm not averse to destabilising the professional storytelling of criticism with a literary pratfall, I'm going to see if I can make this reading stick as an example of embarrassensibility in action. That's to say, performing a reading that ruffles rather than quells or sublimates its embarrassments, and thinking about what the embarrassment of the *poem itself* might be, in relation to conventional language use, and bearing in mind that this may be different again from the embarrassment of the speaker or the reader.

The critical consensus on Bishop, especially among her peers, has been to praise her powers of observation, description and restraint, often as opposed to the more transcendent lyric flourishes of modernist contemporaries like Stevens and Yeats. Bishop's voice is seen as modest, composed and dependably unembarrassed: John Ashbery, for example, describes her poetry as speaking in a 'pleasant, chatty, vernacular tone … calmly and unpoetically', while Robert Lowell also praised it for being 'unrhetorical'. The implication is that we should see Bishop as an exemplar of observational immediacy and precision, or of the micro-narrative perhaps, but probably not of lyrical or metapoetic complexity.

And indeed the opening lines of 'In the Waiting Room' seem to support this perspective, being factual and unflamboyant scene-setting, almost anecdotal. Widely anthologised as it is, there's a great deal of published commentary on this poem, most of which responds to the imperative to see Bishop's work as literal and documentary by kicking off with a narrative account of its 'events'. Lee Edelman, in his excellent essay on Bishop's geography of gender (1985) summarises the consensus that 'the poem presents a young girl's moment of awakening to the separations and the bonds among human beings to the forces that shape individual identity through the interrelated recognitions of community'. So far, so A-level. He continues, 'Critics have felt themselves both able and obliged to summarize the "story," to rehearse the events on which the poem's act of recognition hinges.' Helen Vendler, for example, recapitulates the plot as follows: 'Waiting in a dentist's office, reading the National Geographic, feeling horrified at pictures of savages, hearing her aunt cry out in pain from inside the dentist's room, the child feels vertigo.'

The emphasis here on narratological terms, the sort of story, the plot and so forth does raise the question for me of why the poem should place such pressure on critics to furnish it with a *story*, and one moreover that makes the poem seem rather banal and folksy. It's an interesting question to me as my own misreading, as you may have guessed, turns on this cry, the 'oh' attributed by Vendler and most critics to Aunt Consuelo alone, but which I'd like to claim is a more complex figure and indeed as the embarrassment *of the poem itself*.

But first we might unravel the poem's secondary embarrassments, one of which is the situational one of the child's precocious reading. Lee Edelman observes that the parenthetical and unnecessary statement, 'I could read', really ought to flag up the poem's metatextual reflection on the relationship between reading and the constructing of subjectivity. The adult reading matter—and I think that in 1918 we can consider the anthropological images available in *National Geographic* 'adult' in its euphemistic sense—furnishes carefully choreographed examples of binary oppositions: inside and outside (the volcano), primitive and civilised, human beings and animals or meat, literal and figurative language ('a man slung on a pole' vs. 'Long Pig') and, of course, gender. Elizabeth's identifications vacillate between these: human, civilised, female; this last the axis which throws her into disarray, being 'one of them' in relation to the women available in the poem: 'foolish, timid Aunt Consuelo', cross-dressing Victorian explorer Osa Johnson, and the 'black naked women' whose 'breasts were horrifying'.

The odd, obstructive phrasing of the next line, 'I read it right straight through' (a line I can never read 'straight through' without tripping over the words) describes the speaker's literal embarrassment—'I was too shy to stop'—but also draws attention to 'right' and 'straight' as properties of reading, which is to say fluent, but also correct American moral and heteronormative ways of reading, that resist the sideways glance at black skin, body modification, naked breasts and Osa's unseemly breeches (the homonymic pun on 'breaches' perhaps also too good to overlook). But this gaze nonetheless overspills later (we recall the primary image of the volcano and its contiguity to the spilled surface heat of embarrassment), in Elizabeth's glances at the others in the waiting room, or more precisely, at their lower bodies and crotches: 'I gave a sidelong glance, I couldn't look any higher.' This queering pull of the gaze to the sides of the page and the room itself, a movement of contiguity, confusion and embarrassment, carries over from the visible into the audible, culminating in the hinge of the poem, which is an embarrassing (and quintessentially lyric) *overhearing*: 'Suddenly, from inside, / came an *oh*! of pain ...'

The sound of that syllable 'oh', we already know, and as Bishop also must, is a mark of poetic diction as much as a spontaneous involuntary cry, and indeed it's an unusual choice to denote a cry of pain more commonly inscribed as *ow* or *ouch* maybe *argh*, so there seems something artful about it even as it presents itself as the very emblem of involuntary utterance, embarrassing both for those who utter and those who hear it. Yet Elizabeth tells us she *wasn't* embarrassed or surprised by her aunt's behaviour, as long as she can see it as *her aunt's*, for whom she has already expressed a measure of resigned contempt. What's actually surprising and mortifying is the realisation that it's *her* voice. The literal, narrative or 'proper' reading of this is that in the cry, Elizabeth recognises traces of her own voice, the family women's voice, and is thus inducted into her identity as *that particular Elizabeth*. But in my misreading, which has a poetic rather than narrative temporality—and which is a wobble or maybe an instance of negative capability—Elizabeth really does cry out 'oh' at that same time, not only because 'oh' is a natural exclamation of surprise but because she has in fact also fully identified with the embarrassing aunt and is subject to the empathic shimmer of contagion, whereby the receiver–recipient relation is momentarily undone.

In other words, the 'oh' is at once Consuelo's, Elizabeth's, and the poem's own uncertainty about who is speaking, and from which perspective, from which 'inside': a conceit only possible in poetic rather than narrative language, where that syllable is capable of holding at once pain, contempt, empathic identification, genuine surprise, and the index of, or inauguration into, lyric artifice itself. I might even suggest that this poem takes a sideways glance at Moore's poem of the same year and offers 'oh' as a response, the genuine response of the lyric poem, structurally embedded in a scene, a 'waiting room' of embarrassment into which the genuine may be ushered, with all its sideways glances and refusal to 'look any higher'. And to return to Ben Lerner, this falling away from the pure potentiality of being human into the vicissitudes of being an actual person in a concrete historical situation—'Outside / in Worcester Massachusetts, / were night and slush and cold, / and it was still the fifth / of February, 1918'—is precisely what makes it genuine, embarrassing, lyric poetry.

Transcribed by Swati Singh from a talk given at the 'Against Storytelling' Symposium, Ashoka University, February 2018.

Storytelling and Forgetfulness

Amit Chaudhuri

Years ago, I began to run into the claim that we are all storytellers. Storytelling was evidently a primal communal function for humanity. I was assured that we've been telling each other stories since the beginning of time. I felt a churlish resistance to these proclamations, possibly because one might decide that being human doesn't mean one should subscribe, without discomfiture, to everything the human race is collectively doing at any given point. Storytelling shouldn't be guaranteed an aura simply because humans have been at it from the beginning of history. Of course, part of my unease emanated from the fact that the 'beginning of history' is even more of a wishful invention than the 'end of history' is. It occurs to me that we probably began to hear 'We are all storytellers', as an utterance, from the late 1980s and early 1990s onwards. From the moment one first heard this utterance, one was told it had been made from the beginning of time. As with various things that happened in the age of globalisation, radical shifts in our understanding (of value, for instance) quickly acquired an immemorial air. So, for example, it became increasingly difficult to conceive of a period in history that valued things differently from the way the free market does. Middle-class ideology may have concerned itself with appropriating the universal; the 'now' of the free market appears to have been more preoccupied with recruiting eternity. As a result, the popular-culture term 'all time' gained a new meaning with globalisation; like the assertion 'We have always been storytellers', 'all-time' lists and 'all-time greats' often go back over periods, and are applied to categories (like rock guitarists), that are actually thirty years old.

The disciplinary shifts in the humanities privileging 'storytelling' are too numerous to go into here: I'll only give one example. A historian recently told me that she asks her students to liberate themselves from the constraints of their pedagogy by thinking of the novel and behaving like 'storytellers'. As I said to her, this interpretation of the novel, of course, inadvertently makes imaginative writing, especially fiction, synonymous with storytelling: it's as if looking outside the bounds of scholarly work towards fiction or imaginative prose as a model for loosening constraints must privilege narrative, rather than other aspects of fiction, as being constitutive of the liberations of imaginative writing.

A surfeit of 'We are all storytellers' made me realise that this was not really a primary utterance at all. The primary utterance, if there must be one, is praise or acknowledgement of what makes stories and other things possible: existence, life. By 'life' I mean not what narrative is 'about', but what lies on narrative's periphery. What the earliest texts seem to do is to attempt to find a language with which to both come to terms with and acknowledge—even celebrate—the contingency of the fact of existence. The story, with the human or anthropomorphised animal at the centre, emerges in the aftermath of existence, but, paradoxically, has an air of being recounted and a priori, of already having happened. Existence is neither a priori nor originary; it's a moment of possibility.

In the spirit of investigating whether we were always storytellers, I went back to a canonical text. It's from the first millennium BC: the *Kena Upanishad*. It felt important to go back to it because storytelling has been almost dutifully conflated with non-Western cultures, which themselves are often conflated with orality. Writing and inscription are, on the other hand, an Enlightenment project. Outside the West, in the lap of orality, our mothers and grandmothers have been telling us stories from when we were in the womb. Story, for us, has been an autochthonic method of nutrition. While not denying any of this, it was important to check out a primary text from an incorrigibly storytelling culture. '*Kena*' in the *Kena Upanishad* means 'why', connected to the whys and wherefores of the universe. This poetic statement is from the brief opening section of this *Upanishad* (note that Brahman is not to be confused with Brahma, Brahmin or other similar-sounding words):

> Who sends the mind to wander afar, who first drives life to start on its journey, who impels us to utter these words, who is the spirit ['spirit', as the Sanskritist Heeraman Tiwari pointed out to me, is a Judeo–Christian translation of what he calls, in his translation, an all-pervasive 'element'] behind the eye and the ear ... What cannot be spoken with words, but that whereby words are spoken, know that alone to be Brahman.
>
> What cannot be thought with the mind, but that whereby the mind can think, know that alone to be Brahman the spirit and not what people here adore. What cannot be seen with the eye, but that whereby the eye can see—know that alone to be Brahman. What cannot be heard with the ear, but that whereby the ear can hear; what cannot be withdrawn with breath, but that whereby breath is withdrawn, know that alone to be Brahman.[1]

This comes across not so much as a narrative of creation as an instance of self-reflexivity that is at once curiously tortured and liberating. Its meaning can't be paraphrased, but it *can* be rephrased as a series of questions and replies. 'What can't be thought with the mind? Whatever it is that makes the mind think.' 'What can't be seen with the eye? Whatever it is that makes the eye see.' It's an account that abjures progression on behalf of the self-reflexive, of the assertion that turns upon itself.

Here's an excerpt from the third section:

> The Brahman once won a victory for the Devas. Through that victory of the Brahman, the Devas became elated. They thought, 'This victory is ours. This glory is ours.' The Brahman perceived this and appeared before them. They did not know what mysterious form it was.

---

[1] *The Upanishads*, trans. Juan Mascaró (London: Penguin, 1965), p. 51.

> They said to Fire: 'O Jataveda (All-knowing)! Find out what mysterious spirit this is.' He said: 'Yes.'
>
> He ran towards it and He (Brahman) said to him: 'Who art thou?' 'I am Agni, I am Jataveda,' he (the Fire-god) replied.
>
> Brahman asked: 'What power resides in thee?' Agni replied: 'I can burn up all whatsoever exists on earth.'
>
> Brahman placed a straw before him and said: 'Burn this.' He (Agni) rushed towards it with all speed, but was not able to burn it. So he returned from there and said (to the Devas): 'I was not able to find out what this great mystery is.'
>
> Then they said to Vayu (the Air-god): 'Vayu! Find out what mystery this is.' He said: 'Yes.'
>
> He ran towards it and He (Brahman) said to him: 'Who art thou?' 'I am Vayu, I am Matarisva (traveller of Heaven),' he (Vayu) said.
>
> Then the Brahman said: 'What power is in thee?' Vayu replied: 'I can blow away all whatsoever exists on earth.'
>
> Brahman placed a straw before him and said: 'Blow this away.' He (Vayu) rushed towards it with all speed, but was not able to blow it away. So he returned from there and said (to the Devas): 'I was not able to find out what this great mystery is.'[2]

Although similar in shape and tone to Judeo–Christian parables about miraculous strength, like the one about Samson bringing down the columns, this is really a parable about delicacy. After all, what's at issue here is not moving mountains, but a straw. You don't need strength to move a straw: what is it that you need, then? Delicacy is non-narrative; as with writing a poem, you can't coerce its workings. Narrative and story by themselves are neither the same thing as, nor a guarantee of, movement; this is what writers, like the mystified Devas, need to learn quickly. Otherwise the straw stays inert.

I never liked reading novels. My growing up was spent consuming comic books and poems. I was eventually drawn to novels through

---

[2] Ibid., pp. 52–53.

exceptional paragraphs cited in essays; by my late teens, I was probably more likely to read a piece of criticism about a work rather than the work itself. One such paragraph occurs in *A House for Mr Biswas* by V.S. Naipaul, where Biswas in his early life takes a new job as a sign painter after having been a bus conductor. I encountered it in my early twenties in a critical essay about the book in an anthology on 'Commonwealth Literature'. Biswas must reproduce the edict, 'IDLERS KEEP OUT BY ORDER.'

> ... his hand became surer, his strokes bolder, his feeling for letters finer. He thought R and S the most beautiful of Roman letters; no letter could express so many moods as R, without losing its beauty; and what could compare with the swing and rhythm of S? With a brush, large letters were easier than small ...[3]

I was transfixed by this paragraph, and felt it was a shame that I'd have to read the novel. I was content, instead, to reread the paragraph endlessly. This is because the paragraph presented me with a possibility. The possibility was the novel. The novel I was presented with was not the telling, the recounting, that I would purportedly have to read. That act of reading the narrative, the recounting, would, in a sense, diminish the possibility generated by this encounter with the paragraph. Where, then, are we likely to find this moment of possibility in a piece of writing; in, say (since we are talking about storytelling), a work of narrative fiction? To me it seems it resides in the sort of standalone paragraph such as the one I've quoted, which belongs to a story but is also independent of it, in that it seems equally located in an irreducible life and textuality outside that novel as it is in the life narrated and contained within it.

The moment of possibility resides especially in the opening paragraphs of a work of fiction, or any paragraph that has the irresolution, the air of open-endedness and lifelikeness, the lack of recountedness, that opening paragraphs have. The paragraphs in the first page of a novel (sometimes in the second and third pages too) have not been bound yet by the telling, but are opening out on

---

[3] V.S. Naipaul, *A House for Mr Biswas* (London: Penguin, 1969), p. 76.

to something. My ambition, always, was to write novels composed entirely of opening paragraphs and then to put them in some kind of order. The order would be a sequence that was partly illusory. Of course, we are experts at creating an illusion of continuity, both as readers and writers, and I believe that if you give somebody a text without any narrative they will impose continuity on it. My subterranean aim—so subterranean that it's taken me two decades to see what I was up to—was to create an assemblage of opening paragraphs, to expand as much as possible, without introducing a sense of development, the vivid lack of resolution of the first three or four pages.

What kind of text is produced by an artist who doesn't want the moment of possibility to be closed down by the compulsion or the need to tell? Once you commit to telling, the moment in the opening paragraph is over. We know for a fact that many writers have wonderful opening pages whose magic is sacrificed to higher causes, such as observances to do with the syntax of realism, and the responsibility of portraying the arc of the existence of certain human beings or 'characters': the novelist 'must become the whole of boredom itself', says W.H. Auden, who was in awe of, and slightly bewildered by, this voluntary taking on of the depiction of social milieu almost as a form of social responsibility. This loss of the abandon of the opening pages is characteristic of the human compromise, the deep maturity, that the novel represents, when the writer knowingly assents to being shackled by the need for narrative and telling. Naipaul himself is a fundamental example of a writer who sometimes begins with astonishing passages of lifelikeness, but then not so much loses the plot, or loses himself to a plot, but takes on upon himself fetters that are clearly unwanted. Joan Didion recognises this, and expands on the peculiar sensory excitement of the first three pages of Naipaul's *Guerrillas*, which she confesses to compulsively rereading, almost as if the rest of the novel didn't really matter. In the novella *In a Free State*, Naipaul translates, with extraordinary vitality in the opening section, an intuition of possibility into a story about a European man and woman who must journey urgently and impulsively out of an African country in the time of a coup. Then, like his two characters, he seems not to know what to do except see the journey through. As the syntax of narrative takes over, not only does the representation of the journey feel increasingly entrapping, but also—as is often the case with Naipaul when he feels unhappy—by most standards morally and politically peculiar, turgid, and alienating.

Something similar happens in his travelogue, *An Area of Darkness*.[4] Towards the beginning, a period of waiting is described: the ship, on its way to India, has stopped at the port in Alexandria. Nothing happens; horse-drawn cabs are awaiting fares. Few arrive, and melancholy settles in. This melancholy is a form of excitement, just as the waiting-for-something-to-happen is a kind of energy unmatched by the events later narrated in the book, the actual encounter with India, which is the book's legitimate subject. For Naipaul, as possibility recedes (and possibility, for him, as the chapter on Alexandria shows, has little do with optimism), questionable moral judgement begins to dominate: this is *his* response to the cost of succumbing to narrative propriety—not so much 'becoming the whole of boredom itself', but an alienated chafing.

A House for Mr Biswas opens with a short prologue, where everything is indeterminate and proleptic. It begins, 'Ten weeks before he died, Mr Mohun Biswas, a journalist of Sikkim Street, St James, Port of Spain, was sacked', and then goes on to dwell, for five pages, on Biswas's house, a house that's 'flawed' and 'irretrievably mortgaged': 'during these months of illness and despair he was struck again and again by the wonder of being in his own house, the audacity of it'. We are suspended here, in the prologue, with Mr Biswas, between arrival and departure. Naipaul manages to stay throughout with this sense of the possible, and he does this by constantly returning to Biswas's disbelieving conviction, even at the end of the novel, that the house on Sikkim Street is a house he's just begun to live in: 'In the extra space Mr Biswas planted a laburnum tree.' In my edition, 583 of 590 pages have gone by when this sentence appears; and yet, despite all that has ensued and is now finished, we're still absorbing the prologue's 'wonder' and 'audacity' of arrival.

---

[4] V.S. Naipaul, *An Area of Darkness* (London, André Deutsch, 1964).

Arrival, like existence, and unlike story, lacks the air of the a priori and the narrated. In *The Enigma of Arrival*, the ship that paused at harbour in *An Area of Darkness* appears again, but this time in a de Chirico painting that gives both its title and its atmosphere of lapsed expectancy to the book. Midway through the novel, the narrator reflects that the painting is about a ship that sailed into a city, and a man who got off at the port and intended to go back, but forgot to: 'The antique ship has gone. The traveller has lived out his life.'[5] The inadvertent forgetting of the matter of going back, rather than the creation of a new existence, becomes this person's story, as it does the narrator's. Forgetting and possibility become, then, interchangeable; the life is never really recounted. It—the novel; the painting—doesn't contain the tale of an immigrant; it represents an attempt at immersion in a beginning, what Naipaul calls 'arrival', involving an action endlessly postponed, which the narrator encapsulates with the words, 'The traveller has lived out his life.'

How do we construct a page composed of opening paragraphs? One is reminded, of course, of Walter Benjamin's ambition to write a book composed entirely of quotations. A quotation for him, as in his essays on Kafka, is also a paragraph; for my younger self, for reasons I mentioned earlier, and maybe for my present self too, a paragraph is a quotation. A novel is an assemblage of paragraphs or quotations, which both belong to the narrative and are outside it. A quotation in an imaginative work—say, an essay—causes unsettlement. It's there not as evidence, to legitimise a claim, as it might in a scholarly work, but to remind us that the narrator is distracted, that they've made an association and have been momentarily led from the text to another text outside it. The quote is not wholly present in the narrative; it's partly elsewhere. So the quote doesn't just further an argument; it leads to an opening up. The paragraph, as I understand it, must have the same sense of not being wholly present that the quotation, in Benjamin's sense, does. When Benjamin speaks of his ambition

---

[5] V.S. Naipaul, *The Enigma of Arrival* (London: Penguin, 1987), p. 92.

to write a book composed entirely of quotations, he's speaking of a method of building that brings together units that belong, but also don't wholly belong, to the argument or narrative. A quoted paragraph for him is a standalone paragraph, because it comprises a possibility that makes recounting—that is, the rest of the narrative—redundant. If the paragraph is at least doubly located in fiction, then one location lies in fiction's purported task, the recounting of a life; the other lies outside it, in acknowledging what's more powerful than 'story'—the present's contingency.

I've not forgotten that this piece has to do with 'forgetfulness and storytelling', for which reason I wish to look at the opening section of Kafka's *Metamorphosis* in Michael Hofmann's translation:

> When Gregor Samsa awoke one morning from troubled dreams, he found himself changed into a monstrous cockroach in his bed. He lay on his tough, armoured back, and, raising his head a little, managed to see—sectioned off by little crescent-shaped ridges into segments—the expanse of his arched, brown belly, atop which the coverlet perched, forever on the point of slipping off entirely.
>
> 'What's the matter with me?' he thought. It was no dream. There, quietly between the four familiar walls, was his room, a normal human room, if always a little on the small side. Over the table, on which an array of cloth samples was spread out—Samsa was a travelling salesman—hung the picture he had only recently clipped from a magazine, and set in an attractive gilt frame. It was a picture of a lady in a fur hat and stole, sitting bolt upright, holding in the direction of the onlooker a heavy muff into which she had thrust the whole of her forearm.
>
> From there, Gregor's gaze directed itself towards the window, and the drab weather outside—raindrops could be heard plinking against the tin window ledges—made him quite melancholy. 'What if I went back to sleep for a while, and forgot about all this nonsense?' he thought, but that proved quite impossible, because he was accustomed to sleeping on his right side, and in his present state he was unable to find that position ...

'Oh, my Lord!' he thought. 'If only I didn't have to follow such an exhausting profession! On the road, day in, day out. The work is so much more strenuous than it would be in the head office, and then there's the additional ordeal of travelling, worries about train connections, the irregular, bad meals, new people all the time, no continuity, no affection. Devil take it!' He felt a light itch at the top of his belly ...

He slid back to his previous position. 'All this getting up early,' he thought, 'is bound to take its effect. There are some other travelling salesmen I could mention who live like harem women ... If I didn't have to exercise restraint for the sake of my parents, then I would have quit a long time ago; I would have gone up to the director and told him exactly what I thought of him. He would have fallen off his desk in surprise! That's a peculiar way he has of sitting anyway, up on his desk, and talking down to his staff from on high, making them step up to him very close because he's so hard of hearing.[6]

What's striking is how both Gregor and the narrator have forgotten what the central predicament and theme are, or are incapable of grasping their centrality. Gregor is more concerned with the difficulty of turning on his side in his present state, a difficulty that impedes his plan to sleep a bit longer; he is made melancholy by the sound of rain; he will soon become aware of the unfairness of train schedules; in the meantime, he's incensed by the memory of his boss's posture. Another writer, a lesser writer, wouldn't have permitted this losing sight, so early on, of the immensity of what's happened. But the liberation of the opening pages of *Metamorphosis* comes from their inability to be absolutely present, their vacillation between being in the story of a man who has become a giant insect and their forgetting of this story and their leakage into something outside it: the matter of living, with its timetables and trains, which is supposed to feed its experiences into the story but also competes with and is unconscious of it.

---

[6] Franz Kafka, *Metamorphosis and other stories*, trans. Michael Hofmann (London: Penguin, 2007), p. 73.

There's another kind of forgetfulness here: that of objects, or what in literary works we call 'detail'. The picture of the woman 'sitting bolt upright'; the gilt frame; the coverlet; the tin window ledges; the rain—these seem not to be fully conscious of being part, as background, of a story of a man who finds he's a giant insect. Their role is not even ironical, as, according to Auden, the role of the animals and humans in Breughel's painting of Icarus's fall into the ocean is: 'how everything turns away / Quite leisurely from the disaster'.[7] In *Metamorphosis*, detail is not so much indifferent to the disaster as it is to being in a story about a disaster; its location is both in the story and independent of it. So a narrative with an easily paraphrasable centrality of focus becomes, instead, an example of multiple and dispersed openings out. Its details have their counterpart not in Breughel's *Icarus*, or in realist fiction, or in period or genre cinema, but in Abbas Kiarostami's movies, where non-professionals are often not playing characters but themselves, and aren't fully mindful that they're in a larger story. They're in the film and outside it. The same can be said of animals, air, water and trees in a Tarkovsky film, or in a film like *The New World* by Terence Malick: that all these are non-professional actors unaware of playing the role of the characters 'animal', 'air', 'water', and 'trees' respectively, but are, inadvertently, themselves. They emanate, if you notice them, an innate forgetfulness of the story they're in, as do the paragraphs I've mentioned. In this regard, the details I'm discussing are quite unlike those in period or sci fi films, where objects, horses, elephants and things exude, like the protagonist, an awareness at every point of being either in history or in the future, two easily recognisable categories that embody further modulations on the recounted air of storytelling.

Jean Paul Sartre was intrigued by the idea of the adventure. An adventure, of course, is another name for story: for children, 'adventure story' is a tautology. Here's Sartre's narrator in *Nausea*:

---

[7] W.H. Auden, 'Museé des Beaux Arts', *Selected Poems* (New York: Vintage, 2007), p. 87.

> For the most banal event to become an adventure you must, and this is enough, begin to recount it. This is what fools people. A man is always a teller of tales. He sees everything that happens to him through them and he tries to live his own life as if you were telling a story, but you have to choose, live or tell.[8]

In other words, we don't, can't, know we're in an adventure or in a story. The same can be said of history: no one is really aware of living in a historical epoch. Conversations with people who have participated in historic situations, whether it's a performance by John Coltrane or the partition of a country, confirm this unknowingness: all they recall is what it was like to be present at that time. But forgetfulness is absent from historical novels or films, as it is in films about the future; both the past and the future are assembled by bringing together markers of history—turbans, togas, or forelocks—or the future: spaceships and space. Even space lacks forgetfulness in films like *2001: A Space Odyssey*, whose story is already, a priori, being narrated as the 'future'. Space, in Kubrick's film, becomes a metaphor for the 'homogenous empty time' of history that Benjamin says makes the idea of man's progress possible: the historicism that imbues our notions of the futuristic and historical is enacted succinctly in the film's opening—an ape from a prehistoric epoch flings a bone into the air which, ascending in 'homogenous empty time', becomes a spaceship.

Yet both Kubrick in *Barry Lyndon* and certainly Tarkovsky in historical films like *Andrey Rublov*, or in his science fiction-based cinema, *Stalker* and *Solaris*, reject the notion of the 'adventure'. The 'background' in these movies adheres, on one level, to what Sartre calls 'the most banal event'; for instance, one of the first signals we receive in *Solaris* of dissonance doesn't have to do with science fiction appurtenances, but a horse wandering outside a block of sixties' houses; the second signal, which also comes early, occurs when a tunnel a man is driving through takes inordinately long to end: the tunnel, a very recognisable urban feature (this bit, set in Russia, was apparently shot in Japan, testimony to a certain kind

---

[8] Jean-Paul Sartre, *Nausea* (London: Penguin, 2000).

of mid-century urbanisation available in various cultures), seems to loop in upon itself without in any other way being remarkable. The horses, spaceships, horsemen, and stretches of grass or space in Tarkovsky's films, and in *Barry Lyndon*, possess not identifiable characteristics that mark them out as futuristic or historical, but a disorganised banality, a forgetfulness of the role they're playing in the setting. As a result, both the past and the future are, in these movies, undifferentiated from the non-homogenous present in which we live.

What's the relation between living and telling on the one hand, and between living and writing on the other? The prevalent model for life's relationship to telling is that we live, gather material, and then pour or transform that material experience of living into something that comes out of it: the story we consequently tell.

In my understanding, however, the moment of writing converges with living randomly. There is no decision about transforming into a story material that's been previously experienced or collected; instead, one arrives at a juncture at which there is an unexpected sense of possibility for the writer: I include all of us when I use that word. This sense of possibility comprises what I'm calling 'writing', which need not involve putting pen to paper or sitting down to write an inaugural sentence—as the act is portrayed in Hollywood films, where the 'writer' might be a fictional character or Hemingway or Fitzgerald, poised significantly at the typewriter to start a novel. The physical act of writing, or making that break from life when one sits down to commit oneself to embarking on a work, is a reification, a reduction of the actual intimation of a beginning, a possibility that writing continually constitutes.

Let me give you an example of what I mean. You're looking at the cover of a book and want to own it, to buy it. You study the cover, transfixed by it, and then you don't read the book. You are transfixed not only because you want to read what's contained within, but also because you have begun in a sense to compose or write what's within. The story that's given to you by the book has become secondary to the story you've begun to write. This is the moment of writing. But you have not written anything; you're arrested by what you see on the cover. You buy the book; in fact, you buy many such books, transfixed by them for one reason or another—it could be the jacket or title; it could be your reading, in the bookshop of the first page—and then you put them on the shelf, as a covert gesture towards the perpetual imminence, the possibility, of writing. Your sense of ownership has to do with owning the story, but the story is not to be reduced by recounting, by telling: the story is always to be a possibility, which is why the books on our bookshelves that we don't read outnumber the books that we do. Our bookshelves are largely made up of books that we do not read. These are our ongoing moments of writing—a self-generated accumulation of writing as possibility.

Journalism and the Triumph of the Story

Jeremy Harding

When I started out as a journalist, I had the makings of a very poor one. The pieces I turned in didn't tell proper stories with a beginning, a middle and an end. And I guess—thinking back—they were light on information, even when they were a bit like field reports, about incidents or events. This began to change when I was asked to write by more challenging editors. I remember when it happened. I'd been travelling on the rebel side during the war in Eritrea. It was an independence struggle that set the Eritreans against the colonial regime—as they saw it—in Addis Ababa; it had complicated causes and took many serpentine turns. I believed it was important to explain all this. I felt the need to pack in information. But when the editors got back to me, they said the historical stuff, the background, was too detailed: they found it hard to fight through my thickets of detail. I went over it again, thinning down, and trying not to travesty the story with too many shortcuts. They read it over and now they said they weren't sure they followed: the path was certainly clearer, but it seemed bland and uninflected. What were we to do? So I went back and started re-seeding it with thickets. After more to-ing and fro-ing it was sorted out to everyone's satisfaction. One of the things I came to understand, as I began to write longer descriptive journalism, was that I had a very tenuous sense of structure: I really had none of the narrative prescience that shapes a piece of non-fiction and keeps the reader alongside. I noticed, too, that I tended to think of this overall structure not as an element of composition in itself—you'd have to say an indispensable element—but more as a kind of clothes horse, or a bit of weather-beaten trellis. What mattered was the luminosity of the scenes I could bring to life or the crisp analogies that would allow readers to recognise where they were. And the point, as far as I could tell, was to deck that rickety trellis with as many of these shining moments as I could, without slipping into vulgarity.

The more I had to do with my editors, the better I became at anticipating their objections. And the easier it was to follow their crucial rule: tell me a story. Practicality was the order of the day, or a good part of it. And it dawned on me as I worked my way into storytelling that I'd never thought of writing—even rudimentary kinds of writing—as an activity that served any purpose other than its own. To talk of 'practicality' is to think of writing as a tool for communication, but also a process that eventuates in an outcome beyond the text itself, like a battlefield message from brigade headquarters, or a writ from a lawyer. I was too caught up with the sensuousness of words, their mobility, their playful disposition.

And perhaps at a young age I already sensed the materiality of language—I'd never have called it that, of course—and maybe, as I grew older, the forceful, almost physical impression that language made on me obscured the fact that it is the defining social medium that shapes us all. Not that I'd have put it like that either, but like everybody, I was party to the many ways it went about this shaping: definitions, descriptions, pinning things down, all the tasks that journalism—for example—is supposed to perform.

And like everybody else, I was already woven *in*, from infancy. I'm borrowing the image of weaving from an essay by Heidegger, 'The Way to Language'.[9] There's a terrific passage where he suggests that as speaking persons, we are always part of something larger. 'Language itself,' he writes, 'has woven us into its speaking.'

Two points about this weaving in—a notion I find very helpful: First, is there anywhere better to belong than in language? It's a fabulous expanding cradle in our early years, which evolves into a labile home, and then into a city you know intimately, even though

---

[9] The final essay in *Unterwegs zur Sprache* (1959), trans. David Farrell Krell in his edition of Heidegger's *Basic Writings* (London: Routledge, 1978).

it reconfigures around you at every turn. It's a world that's always yours and always everybody else's, a proper commons, a kind of 'us'. All the same, I think Heidegger's image, the idea of an enormous multidimensional weaving, is better than any I've come up with here.

The second point: I wonder if storytelling doesn't diminish the glory of this rich fabric and our place in it. One way stories can do that is to lay it flat on the ground, like a kind of chequerboard, and then invent gods and mortals, who charge all over it, square to square, according to the laws of destiny. Another is to abstract a handful of filaments from the weave and attach them to 'characters' so that temperament, action and motive seem to have precedence over the medium in which we encounter them. Or rather, they tend to make the medium inconspicuous, as if it didn't really exist.

If I'm puzzled by my second point about the high-handedness of storytelling, or suspect I've tied myself in knots, it's because the modernist writers whose work I admire—and I'd start with Laurence Sterne, born two hundred years before the early modernist appearance of the unreliable narrator—could also be thought of as un-pickers of the Heideggerian weave. But I suspect that the modernists were more interested in playing ingeniously across the warp, with formal surprises, deferrals, intervals in the fabric which make it look more like crochet than weaving. And whether these stories come to us in fine circumlocutions (Henry James) or rich associative movements of the mind across the surface of a self (Virginia Woolf), or ellipsis and ominous mumbling (Conrad), the effect is to privilege the medium over the 'message'. So it's possible, I'd suggest, for novelists to depart from the way a story 'ought' to be told, and fold us even more fully into language, as poets have to. And, of course, to remind us that language is all around us, that we're of it, and that as readers we renew our sense of this belonging in the presence of inventive, unfamiliar forms of discourse.

But I'm taking this further than I meant to. Because if we want the medium to be palpable, we could well end up favouring the idea that 'it is language which speaks, not the author'. I'm quoting, of course, from Roland Barthes's famous essay in the 1960s on the death of the author—an idea triggered, incidentally, less by the prose of Balzac than the verse of Stéphane Mallarmé.[10] But one of the things that's meant here by 'language speaking' is that books, stories, poems are susceptible to endless readings, and that the reader is the arbiter and maker—the sublime re-creator—in the realm of literature.

Saying that language speaks and not the author isn't the same as saying that we're woven—all of us, readers and writers—into whatever language does when we perform it, or it performs us. And it can't be fair to say about good storytellers that their agency is like ... basically footling in the greater scheme of things. Who says there can't be writing that tells good stories and alerts us to the operations of the medium itself?

But good, well-plotted stories can set off in a direction that readers may not always want to take. We might not want a window onto a perfectly intelligible landscape; and we might not want to read a story in which language becomes invisible in the telling, a story in which plotting and artful organisation are doing so much work that we seem to be having an out-of-body experience as we read—transported, as people used to say, taken out of ourselves and maybe also feeling we're no longer woven in.

At a young age I had a couple of counter-intuitive insights about the density of language. The one I'll describe here—please be warned—has to do with sex. My very odd grandmother used to have a gardener, a beautiful man in his forties, and this gardener worked around my grandmother's ramshackle house, doing a lot more than gardening: he looked after the pump that drew the water from her well, changed the mantles on her gas lamps, repaired the roof and all the rest. Often he worked with a boy in his teens called Richard.

Richard was the son of a local artisan—his dad was a plumber. And this Richard of mine thought it was a good idea to tell me about sex. Which, I mean, it probably was, and he set about this task with a grand, didactic passion. I was about six, I think. There was a stand of trees where my grandparents kept a rusting tractor, behind the

---

[10] Written in 1967 and translated by Stephen Heath in *Image-Music-Text*, an anthology of Barthes's essays (London: Fontana, 1977).

gardener's sheds, and that's where these tutorials took place, over a couple of afternoons. They had three elements:

1) description: anatomy of the mature adult;
2) narrative: motives, actions and outcomes (first ... and then ... and then ... and eventually);
3) crucially, they contained new, unfamiliar vocabulary.

I was allowed to ask questions and no doubt I did. But when I thought about these revelations in the evenings, as you would, I remember cycling through the descriptive and narrative elements in short order. They made a kind of straightforward sense, take it or leave it. I also remember settling down to meditate at length on the new vocabulary, its almost physical weight and its terseness, with words of one syllable doing a lot of the work.

Like every anglophone child, I was fascinated by the prevalence of certain vowel-sounds in this tour d'horizon of sexual activity between humans. But for reasons I can't explain I was even more intrigued by the consonants. I was so curious about the new profanities I'd learned—and felt such growing confidence in my mastery—that when I played around with them in my mind, I wondered whether Richard could have got some of them wrong: I began substituting consonants and consonant blends, either side of the vowel sounds, to see if the words sounded more plausible. At the same time, I'm sure, thinking back, that it was the repetition of these words, rather than Richard's description and narrative, that persuaded me I'd understood what he was trying to explain.

I realise that, in this symposium 'against storytelling', I've just told you a story.

But a child can't depend on the sensuous encounter with words to accede to the world: that little person also needs narratives—even partisan, ideological narratives that can be discarded later—and she needs descriptions, whether they're accurate or wide of the mark. The same is true for anyone trying to apprehend in detail whatever lies beyond their own direct experience. I can test what I'm saying—and I'm sure I'm not the first—when I look at Dürer's famous woodcut of a rhinoceros. The creature itself was a gift to a Portuguese colonial governor in Gujarat. And the governor shipped this tragic animal to Lisbon in the year 1515. It was an early imperialist trophy.

Dürer never set eyes on the rhinoceros. But it would have been impossible, simply by repeating its name over and over to himself—punning and playing around with the word *rhinocerus*—for a draughtsman to come up with a reasonable likeness. Possibly, Dürer saw some sort of sketch; we know for sure that he worked from at least one description drafted in Lisbon. Even so, it requires craft, imagination, and a modicum of information, for a person to represent a thing they've never set eyes on with a measure of accuracy. Nowadays we'd say it's about data. The right Artificial Intelligence programme could do it without much difficulty.

Part of my ambivalence about storytelling comes from the feeling that we already have the data. We know how a story might go, and how it's set up to conceal the machinery of telling that's at work: we've acquired this familiarity through a long, trans-generational assimilation of a literary past, and other traditions as well: nursery rhymes, puppet shows, musicals, Hollywood movies. In a sense we know by heart how stories work and how descriptions are made; what things look like in the world of the story and how they behave. And for all these reasons we no longer really need to flesh out the rhinoceros again—a reiteration of a reiteration—at least not in works of fiction. And it follows, I guess, that we've also learned to anticipate what language is being asked to do—moving around incognito, shifting the scenery as discreetly as possible. Or being foregrounded from time to time to embody a character's voice or inhabit a narrator.

I'm in awe of this stage-managing if it's discreetly done. Yet don't we sometimes feel impatient, as the basics of storytelling are rehearsed with each exemplary production? As though we'd agreed not to notice, or to cover our eyes as a prop was dragged into position? Aren't we sometimes restless when we find we know how something will end? And only vaguely appeased by a clever sequence of twists? And what of the problem of getting through the first three chapters of a book and beginning to see the movie or the TV version?

Where did we get this knowingness? It's not an advantage for a reader to see *through* writing. I'm convinced it's a curse. But we are where we are, our sensibilities still defined by certain strains of modernism. It's a bit like carrying a virus whose symptoms keep reappearing. I recognise we're in dangerous territory here: I've just used the M-word again and I could take us onto even more shaky terrain by talking about 'experimental' writing. Still, there is—or was—a sort of modernism that forces us to 'see through', and perhaps 'see beyond' the machinery of storytelling. And open ourselves up to different challenges—eventually different pleasures.

The modernist writers who typify this knowingness have a disruptive interest in the formal properties of texts and indeed, in the habits of usage (here, I suppose, is the sense in which we could call them un-pickers of language, but I'd prefer to think of them as ambitious Penelopes whose every revision or refusal adds to the whole). Obviously, I'm not referring here to a modernism that makes radical claims about the human condition—the modernism of D.H. Lawrence, say, or—at the opposite pole—Kafka. This kind of storytelling observes most of the formal protocols; its power resides in 'the content', as people used to say. I mean a more self-conscious, experimental writing—writing driven by what Gertrude Stein called an 'excess of consciousness'.

Hyper-consciousness, I guess, is a better term, a tremendous attention to the world and the materials at a writer's disposal, language above all, since the medium *is* the material. Then, too, there is the process of perception itself—what it is to know or to see—and the challenge of representing things afresh. Pound thought of this as making it new. Gertrude Stein herself is a good example; and there's no shortage of poets—including Hilda Doolittle—who made it new—then a little later the Objectivists, including Lorine Niedecker, on and across to Black Mountain and up through the 1960s. This approach assumes we're already familiar with the going conventions of various genres, and that we'll have no trouble when we encounter ellipsis ... juxtaposition ... the gleaming fragment. But if the going gets hard, the texts seem to imply, then perhaps we need to put in more imaginative and intellectual work.

There's another important strand, which you might call 'blockbuster eclectic': a lusty, highly ingestive approach which puts pressure on the boundaries of the text until they give way and we find ourselves in a glorious tangle of ideas and registers, and a complicity of genres. Men are better than women at this monumental 'excess of consciousness', which is why it's a visible tradition from very early on; think of Rabelais, and later of Sterne and *Tristram Shandy* (1759–1767), move forward a century to Melville (*Moby-Dick*, 1851) and ahead again to *Ulysses* (1922). We could talk later about why Proust, for all his loquaciousness, doesn't fall into this garrulous modernist lineage. Or why Beckett, sparse as his work became, seems to be perched at the edge of it. Of course, there's every shade of in-between, and many overlaps.

For richer or poorer, I'm 'woven in'—as a reader—by these disruptive, surprising ways of telling stories. The more I try to compose coherent stories, as journalists must, the stronger my affection for stories that resist straightforward tellings, and tellings that stray from the stories we thought they were about to unfold for us. There are plenty of these around now, some of them written by people taking part in this symposium. It only enhances the stature of these authors when I say that I hear language speaking itself as they write.

Let me break off and read here.

My first extract is from Deborah Levy's 'living autobiography', part 2, *The Cost of Living* (2018). We're into a passage about grief, and an allusion to *Hamlet*, that turns back to an address by Levy, or some kind of narrator, to the mother she's mourning. We start with a quotation from Act 2, scene 2 of *Hamlet*, and go on from there:

Words, words, words
I think he's trying to say that he's inconsolable. *(The he is Hamlet)*

Words can cover up everything *(the narrator goes on)*
I don't see ghosts but I can *hear* you listening

The war is over for you.

Here's some news from the living. I have been visited by birds all this year, in one way or another. Some of them are real and some of them are less real.

and a beat further on:

I've stopped thinking about why I'm obsessed with birds but it might be to do with death and renewal.

The second extract is from something Amit Chaudhuri wrote. I thought at first to quote from an intriguing passage in his novel *Friend of My Youth* (2017), where the narrator is interviewed by a journalist and talks about what fiction is and what it does. But Chaudhuri wrote something else in a piece for *Granta* that's closer to what I'm trying to get at today.[11] He was thinking back over revisions he did on drafts of his first novel, *A Strange and Sublime Address* (1991). He tells us he found the process painful. In 'the second phase of revision', he explains, he decided not to establish linking passages 'between one salvaged bit and another. I arranged paragraphs that had no innate sequentiality in order to give them an appearance of linearity. Each participated in, and ignored, the onward current.'

We're almost talking here about the evolution of a modernist canvas, with elements disposed according to the shifting rules of composition. I'll take a chance and say that what Chaudhuri describes is not unlike the way in which Pound recast *The Waste Land* as a sequence of fragments. And because this kind of approach to composing is far from dead and buried I've begun to think that I completely misunderstood what happened to storytelling in the 1980s. At the time, I believed it was the end of everything that interested me. I came to the view that we'd all been forced back onto an idea of 'nature'. Ultra-liberal market theories in the Reagan/Thatcher era suggested that we were indeed part of the animal kingdom. And that the new vision of political economy was thoroughly 'natural'.

---

[11] 'First Sentence', *Granta*, online edition, 22 June 2017.

Everything seemed suddenly to have been naturalised. Even in sport, 'force of nature' came to seem as indispensable as skill. And suddenly modernism's habit of turning the mirror away from nature to look at representation itself appeared to be decadent.

In the 1980s, we saw a flurry of neo-classicism in architecture, a conservative retreat in jazz and—in quite a lot of fiction—a return to the fully naturalised story that seems to mirror the 'real': good narrative arc, true-to-life characters, exemplary use of perspective. Something like a life class. That coincided, by the way, with a vogue for travel writing: the well-meaning white man was venturing out again among 'remote' peoples to test the truths which unregulated free-market capitalism claimed to understand. But the point I kept missing was just how resilient those modernist strands I'd thought were severed actually turned out to be.

In the 1980s, I was living in New York. I was befriended briefly by Kathy Acker. Over a couple of months we played two, maybe three games of chess in her apartment, a bolted bunker-like affair whose whereabouts I've forgotten, maybe somewhere around Gramercy Park. During our first game I thought: if I lose this, she'll cast me into outer darkness. And moments later: what if I win? But her apartment already felt like outer darkness to a sheltered European like myself. New York was in many ways the place I feared to be: so many modernisms seemed passé or insignificant, dwarfed above all by the ultra-liberal politics of the period, a crushing blow to the very idea of a literary avant-garde. And yet my generous host, who took to me because I was a waif in the city, was an avant-gardista of the first water, even if I never grasped what she was doing in her novels. Or what her marginal books—as they seemed to me then—would amount to. But I do now. 'There is no master narrative,'[12] she wrote years later, 'nor realist perspective' to adumbrate 'social and historical facts'. And so she'd just gone on writing because there was always a 'real' in need of inventing.

The business of writing, the narrator tells us in Chaudhuri's *Friend of My Youth*, 'is not about life. It is a form of living. The two happen

---

[12] Kathy Acker, *Pussy, King of the Pirates* (New York: Grove Press, 1996).

simultaneously.' I can see that. And there's something else: the writing I make sense of best is also a conspicuous form of thinking. It's almost as if I was following the movement of thought itself. Restless and elliptical or fluent and discursive ... jagged bursts with curious interruptions, or alternatively a constant, gentle pressure like a breeze coming off the hills. If poems can do this, so can prose. That includes stories that are often about their own making: scavenging, allusive, Ackerist projects that aren't quite the same as storytelling.

I know, as I'm talking, that I'll have to start writing a story of my own a day or so from now. That's journalism. It'll be as clear and economical as I can make it. It will spell out as many difficulties as I think need spelling out. My editor will send me back to make a passage more explicit. Perhaps the piece will have to be cut to fit the page. Someone, possibly me, will introduce a spelling mistake in a last-minute change. It's a working life and I really enjoy it for most of the time. But when I take a break and turn to a book for pleasure—maybe two weeks from now—what will I want to read? Will I go for a conventional work of fiction—maybe a rollicking story? Because for all I've said today, I can find myself immersed and impressed by a compelling narrative, with its mastery of all those not-so-secret arts.

But what if the curse of knowingness descends again and I see through it? This risk is always present when I find myself in front of a well told tale. So perhaps I'll go for a different kind of book, and a different order of artifice, which won't be aiming to sweep me off my feet: something writerly that will reassure me that I'm woven in, as the author explores the vast fabric of language and I hear the reassuring clack of shuttles working back and forth.

UP Against Storytelling,
for David Antin[13]

Charles Bernstein

≤≥÷∫√≈Ω.

          I told my
          wife,
          I
          don't want
          any more
          stories,
          tell me what
          you need.

---

[13] As mentioned at the beginning of this book, the first version of this work was presented at the 'Against Storytelling' symposium on 24 February 2018. The symposium was organised by Amit Chaudhuri and held at the India International Centre in New Delhi, sponsored by Ashoka University and the University of East Anglia (UK). A sound recording of my talk, entitled 'Against Storytelling / Before Time, for David Antin' was published by Obieg (Warsaw) in *Art & Literature: A Mongrel's Guide*, edited by The Book Lovers (David Maroto and Joanna Zielińska). The recording concludes with a coda called *Now Time*—a sound version of the final section, made especially for this publication. *Obieg* also published the handwritten cards I used as my notes for the talk. In presenting the talk, I shuffled the cards to create a disjunct order, meant to interrogate Antin's distrust of parataxis. At a memorial event for Antin at Artists Space on 27 March 2018, I presented another version of the talk, this time with PowerPoint slides randomly arranged, called 'Up Against Storytelling'. A bilingual version was published as *Speaking and Listening and En Parlant, En Ecoutant* by Shelter Press at La Criée Centre d'Art Contemporain in Rennes, France. For links and media files, go to PennSound <writing.upenn.edu/pennsound/x/Bernstein-talks.php#Dehli>. Thanks to Peter Middleton, Marjorie Perloff, and Amit Chaudhuri, Susan Bee and Julien Bismuth.

I told
my husband, I
don't
want any
more stories,
tell me what you
think.
I told my
mother, I
don't
want any
more of
your stories, just
tell
me what
you want.
I
told
my father,
I
don't
want
any more
of
your stories,
just
tell me
where I
went wrong.
I told my
rabbi, I
don't
want any
more of your
God-damn
stories, just

tell
me
how to
get out of here.
I told
my friend, I
don't want
any
more stories, just
tell me
what's
going on.
I told
my professor,
I
don't want
any more
stories,
just tell
me you'll
stop.
I
told my president,
I
don't want
any more
stories,
just get
your foot off
my face.

¶·§ BLT (#BigLieTrump)
In the aftermath of popular-vote-loser Trump's election, the search for blame began. In some accounts, the blame laid on

postmodernists and poststructuralists who had so undermined truth that now a president is free to lie with impunity.[14] As a professional sophist, I am used to the charge. Like the marshal said to the sheriff, 'It comes with the territory.'

Questioning the essential truthfulness of stories—the jargon of storytelling—including journalistic stories is always provocative and it's best when it's meant to be: not shutting down the views of others but getting more voices into the agora. (No, *agora* is not deep muscle pain treatable by Ben-Gay: Get real!) The *opposite* of Trump's univocal embrace of the *truth in my lies* is the sophist's *lies in my truth*, what Jerome McGann calls 'truth in the body of falsehood'. For every Trump lie chronicled by reporters, there is a Trump counterclaim of the 'lying media'. This is Trump's biggest trap, his claim to the moral high ground. Trump appropriates the mantle of truth, insisting that those who disagree are the liars because they deny the truth not only of his story but also the truth of stories. Indeed, Large Sectors of the Massed Media (LSMM) find themselves on precarious ground in calling Trump out, given their almost religious devotion to the truth of stories. There is a history here going back in America from Chautauqua, the nineteenth-century platform for preachers, entertainers and self-help gurus right up to today's Ted Talks, and clones, which scrub away any narrative shards on NPR's airwaves. But this American life is more than an endless drone of hyperfascinating stories.

Hyperfascination, as William Burroughs might say, is a virus, but not from outer space, from inner space.

The problem is not Trump or any individual. Trump is a synecdoche.

---

[14] See, for example, Thomas Edsall's summary, 'Is President Trump a Stealth Postmodernist or Just a Liar?', *The New York Times*, 25 January 2018, https//www.nytimes.com/2018/01/25/opinion/trump-postmodernism-lies.html.

111.

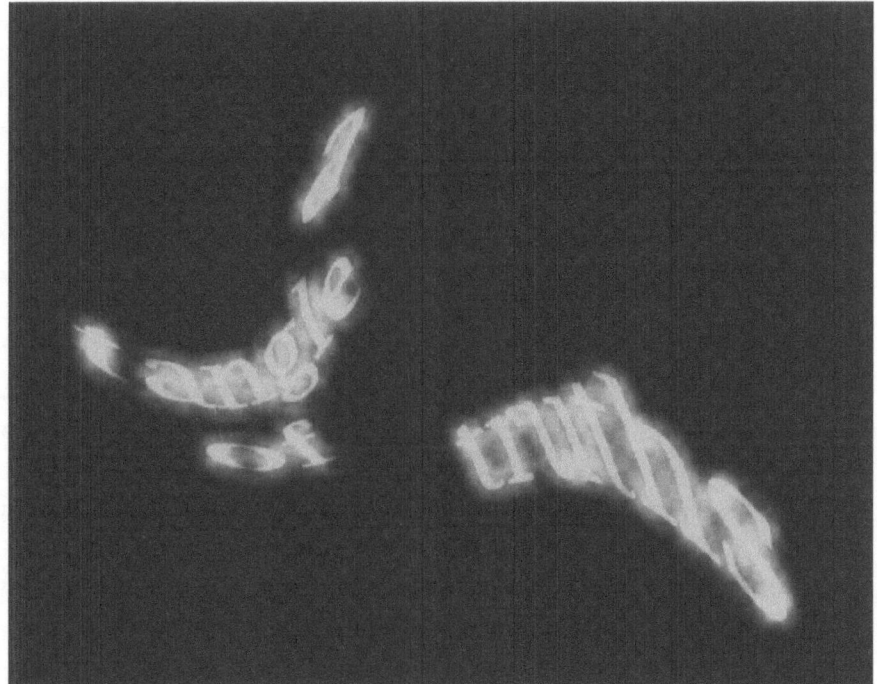

15. Amit Chaudhuri

About a decade ago, I interrupted a talk I was giving to a small group of international writers and academics gathered in Delhi to say, 'Fuck storytelling.'

My respondent, a British Asian literary journalist, later said, while commenting on my talk, how 'shocked' she'd been by my remark. It wasn't the expletive she objected to, but my attack on 'storytelling', which had been so 'empowering to peoples and cultures'. 'Storytelling' had, by now, become a sacred cow that you insulted at your own risk.

My discomfiture with the idea that 'storytelling' is a feature of non-Western culture, and a valuable resource, as a result, of a postcolonial politics that sets itself up against the Enlightenment. A glance at non-Western artistic expression reveals, however, a deep commitment to forms outside of what we now think of as 'narrative' (synecdoche, for instance, and other means of poetic elision) ... Globalisation, by the turn of the millennium, had become a kind of narrative—a lateral, interconnected network from which there was no escape, and from which no one evidently desired to escape—and this privileging of a narrative that had no 'outside' (globalisation) led to the marginalisation of the poetic ... 'Storytelling', with its kitschy magic and its associations of postcolonial empowerment, is seen to emanate from the immemorial funds of orality in the non-Western world, and might be interpreted as a critique of the inscribed word, and its embeddedness in Western forms of knowledge.[15]

¶¶§∞¶•∞.

The New York Times was soft on confronting the facts of the Cold War, successions of US government invasions, the shift of capital to the one per cent, the Bloombergisation of Manhattan. *The Times* spent the 2016 election tip-toeing around Trump's lies. Post election, they rolled out a slogan—'Truth. It's more important now than ever.' But you have to wonder why it wasn't just as important before the election, or during the Iraq invasion. Then there's another new *Times* slogan, 'Truth has a voice'. Is that what truth has? Yes, of course, the *Times* means it offers fact-based journalism, and as a lifelong devoted reader, I am grateful for that. But is that the same as truth? The most important thing is not 'the fact itself' (to echo Kant) but *which facts and how they are constellated*—an ensemble that creates both meaning and truth. Here's how the *Columbia Journalism Review* put it:

> We believe that the volume of reporting around fake news, and the role of tech companies in disseminating those falsehoods, is both disproportionate to its likely influence in the outcome of the election and diverts attention from the culpability of the

---

[15] Posted on the literary activism website: https://www.literaryactivism.com/against-storytelling-mission-statement/. In his statement, and also in his talk at the conference, Chaudhuri debunks the claim that 'storytelling' is an essential feature of third-world cultures, characterising this claim as a form of romantic primitivism, fostered by postcolonial politics, which makes a false opposition between authenticity and Enlightenment. Chaudhuri's essay was published in the *Los Angeles Review of Books* (20 September 2019) as 'Storytelling and Forgetfulness', lareviewofbooks.org/article/storytelling-and-forgetfulness.

mainstream media itself ... It seems incredible that only five out of 150 front-page articles that *The New York Times* ran over the last, most critical months of the election, attempted to compare the candidate's policies, while only 10 described the policies of either candidate in any detail.[16]

In other words, despite its high-minded ads, *The Times* goes for softcore 'plot'—storylines are addictive—over hard-core narrative.

The pervasive focus on Trump's lies by the mediocracy, including late-night comedy—the more outrageous the lies, the more attention—distracts from his government's actions and positions, including deregulation, the crippling of workers' rights and safety nets, and the wanton abandon of environmental care in the service of transferring wealth and power from the many to the fewer and fewer as well as the US's shameful incarceration rates, especially for African Americans. This focus on Trump's lies also has another effect—echoing the lies, all the while galvanising Trump's base. And yet the mediocracy is trapped, by its own protocols, into not only reporting but also highlighting whatever Trump and his Republican Party enablers say. To echo David Antin's old friend George Lakoff: The repetition of a lie, even when it is labelled a lie, reinforces it.

There is an undeniable, and totally justified, urge to defend the mainstream media against Trump's assaults, to see it as us against them (and I include myself in this). But this elides the media's (and my own) no doubt unintended complicity with Trump. When we fail to consider our own structural faults, Trump chalks up another win.

Trump plays P.T. Barnum to mainstream journalism's all-day sucker. And the social media chorus spreads the virus like zombies in *Dawn of the Dead*.

‡‡∞§§. If Socrates Was a Poet

One of my multiple and conflicting commitments as a writer is to collage as reframing. I am drawn to unexpected swerves that

---

[16] Duncan J. Watts and David M. Rothschild, 'Don't blame the election on fake news. Blame it on the media', *Columbia Journalism Review*, 5 December 2017, cjr.org/analysis/fake-news-media-election-trump.php.

heighten contradictions. In my poetics, disjunction is a means to more intense connections. Interruption and disruption heighten the experience of the verbality of language, so that you are not just subjected to rhetorical devices but get to see and hear them pop, like firecrackers on Independence Day.

David Antin's suspicion of collage, parataxis, and metonymy allowed him to create an essential body of work that pushed back against the reflexive use of parataxis. I share with Antin the sense that collage is a troubled legacy of modernism (as are all legacies). Antin's disapprobation pushes me to make sure that my use of my favourite poetic devices doesn't fall prey to the arbitrary and entropic, sugared by the lure of an attractively dissonant surface. The kind of poetry I want averts the asemic in pursuit of n-dimensional semantic hedonia (n/SH).

I value poetry that has the transformation Antin finds in narrative, that often goes missing in story or plot. Antin's counter-intuitive distinction between story and narrative is similar to the difference between fragmentation as an end in itself ('isolate flecks', to use a phrase of William Carlos Williams) and what Walter Benjamin calls *constellation*. I prize poetry and essays, such as Antin's, in which the parts resonate with one another, beyond just logical or metric connection. But I also want poetry and essays that realise an echopoetics by apparently anti-narrative means.[17]

In a 26 March 2003 talk poem for the Poetics Program at Buffalo called 'War', archived by PennSound, Antin makes a strong case against metonymy and elision, what he calls in the talk 'edge to edge relations', using as his example then-President Bush's linkage of '9/11' with 'weapons of mass destruction' with 'Saddam Hussein', to justify the recent invasion of Iraq:

> if ... you imagine that metonymy connects things that are associable with each other   and you can imagine that metonymy

---

[17] See Jerome McGann's discussion of 'anti-narrative' versus 'non-narrative' in his essay 'Contemporary Poetry: Alternate Routes', in *Politics and Poetic Value*, published as *Critical Inquiry* 13, no. 3 (1987). McGann situates my work as anti-narrative, actively opposing the convention of narrative, in the tradition of Blake.

is what governs   the principle of collage   you are assuming essentially that all the things next to each other   obtain their meaning from their juxtapositions   but is that true? ...   are they related to their referential character   or to their significational character? ...   synecdoche works on very different principles than metonymy   metonymy is part-to-part relations   and the other is part-to-whole relations   part-to-part relations can be an infinite chain   you know, like butter   milk   churn   my aunt Tilda ...   bees   I was stung   a bear at the blueberry bush   you know all these things could come up one after another   in a metonymic chain   and contact between them seems to be missing   although it seems to be filled with the possibility of narrative interpolation   it may be that that is what makes it work   so, I guess when George Bush uses metonymy   to connect Saddam Hussein   with 9/11, what he imagines you will do   is fill it with a scoop of desperadoes   all under Saddam Hussein's order [My transcription.]

Jews/parasites, the Nazi Big Lie, is the locus classicus of this type of malefaction, where 'Jews' can readily be replaced by any designated threat. Trump's signature series—Hussein/Obama/Birther—is a terrifying example. Elision erases the connective tissue of discourse—how you get from one place to another. 'You can drive a whole army' through the gaps, says Antin. It is not that he is advocating the logical relation of each element in a narrative, but rather that his talking cure insists on visceral contiguity over and against deliberate discontinuity, erasure and jump cutting.

In Antin's great talk poems, digression, anecdote and association are favoured over disconnection, fragmentation and dissociation. The gaps in the talk poems mark pauses in an improvised talk (a bit like Charles Olson's 'breath' lines). Antin's gaps eschew erasure and allow for rhythm, allowing for what he calls 'radical coherency'. Above all, like many of his fellow New American poets, and following Dewey, Antin valued process over craft and revision. As Antin famously put it, 'if robert lowell is a poet   i dont want to be a poet   if robert frost was a poet i dont want to be a poet   if socrates was a poet   i'll consider it.'[18] Antin's talk poems invite you to think with them, in dialog, as they are being composed. They don't convey a fixed, predetermined meaning or plot or story. Rather, they allow for what Chaudhuri calls 'deliberate irresolution.'[19]

Still, there is a fundamental difference between eliding the gaps and accentuating them; that is, between 'Big Lie' metonymy and metonymy used to break such viral associations. Just as there is, for Antin, a crucial difference between story (a logical series of plot points) and narrative (which averts closure as a means of grappling with experience). Consider, for example, Ron Silliman's exemplary articulation of disarticulations in *Ketjak* and *Tjanting*. Silliman does not naturalise his disjunctions but rather brings the structure of disjunction into view. He is using 'non-narrative' or para-narrative means to narrative ends, as McGann puts it.

6.

∞=∩∇∉⋠. A House Is Not a Home

In the New Delhi 'Against Storytelling' symposium, Amit Chadhuri made the distinction between a single story and a house, suggesting an even more fundamental distinction between a 'house' and a 'home' but also between 'story' and 'history'. A series of plot points, like a flurry of tweets, might make a story but not the network of connected elements that is a history.

---

[18] David Antin, *Radical Coherency: Selected Essays on Art and Literature 1966 to 2005* (Chicago: University of Chicago Press, 2011), p. 273.
[19] Amit Chaudhuri, *The Origins of Dislike* (Oxford: Oxford University Press, 2018), p. 62.

In his essay 'The Beggar and the King', David Antin argues for a fundamental difference between story and narrative.[20] A plot or story, Antin says, is a 'sequence of events', while a narrative involves a 'transformation'—a transformation that, Antin intimates, entails an aversion of closure. Story or plot 'is about making sense', creating from its elements 'a temporal whole'. In contrast, narrative 'explains nothing' because it makes present an 'experiential' dimension that defies 'intelligibil[ity]'. Indeed, closure, the plot, may well obstruct narrative's 'incommensurability and unintelligibility'.

According to Antin, a story, as for example a news story, leaves the individual plot elements as is: it is a set of facts, real or imagined. Narrative transforms those individual elements into something else, something fundamentally different than in their initial articulation.

When story becomes narrative, there is a reckoning and a price to pay. There is a 'threat and terror of a narrative which could if experienced transform' one beyond one's 'own recognition', as when a beggar become king or Oedipus recognises what he has done.[21]

Antin's contrast of story and narrative is reflected in his preference for live improvised performance of a poem (the talk poem) over reading a set text (the poetry reading). The talk poem allows for what, in *Sense of Walden*, Stanley Cavell calls 'the conditions of our present'. (Cavell's readings of classic Hollywood films are a primer in how to read those works not simply as entertaining yarns but as narratives, in the sense Antin means.)

House/home, story/history, plot/narrative, fragmentation/constellation. *Book*, in Edmond Jabès's sense. I think also of Freud's contrast between melancholy, which obsessively seeks (and fails to find) rational intelligibility, and mourning, which acknowledges unintelligible loss.

---

[20] Antin, 'The Beggar and the King', in *Radical Coherency*. Initially published in *Pacific Coast Philology*, 30, no. 2 (1995): 261–64, 266, 270.

[21] Antin, 'The Price', in *How Long Is the Present: Selected Talk Poems of David Antin*, ed. Stephen Fredman (Albuquerque: University of New Mexico Press, 2014). Antin first staked out the difference between story and narrative in this 1986 talk poem.

David Antin, 'Sociology of Art':

> ... now in a written work   it would have been very easy to go back   erase the false step ...   / but the iliad is not a written work   and there are some things fundamentally different about an oral poem one thing in particular   the technique of erasing i mean in a literary poem theres a text and a determined reader can flip the pages back over and over again   and there is something of an illusion of spatial form   the idea that you can have it there   all at once   lying under your hands   leading to the notion of elegant spatial arrangement and its contraries   clumsy arrangements   all based on fantasies of some spatial existence   that is the result of the minds   deceiving itself into forgetting that it has itself constructed this 'space' and the 'form' that is an imaginary configuration within it   by mere flipping of pages and taking this synthetically derived memory   produced by constant reavailability   and confusing it with real memory   it is this 'constructed' literal form which requires the mechanical operations of erasure and excision   the only way you can get rid of an object is to destroy it   but an oral poem has no such problem   if you take a wrong turn   make a false start   you cant 'erase' it   but you can recover and you can obliterate it from memory   /   you can take advantage of the weakness of human memory by extending through time some kind of   diversionary brilliance[22]

CVC. The Book of Ezekiel
The darkness has its secrets
which light does not know.
It's a kind of perfection,
while every light
distorts the truth.[23]

---

[22] David Antin, 'Sociology of Art', in *Talking at the Boundaries* (New York: New Directions, 1976).

[23] Nissim Ezekiel, 'Hymns in Darkness: XII', in *Collected Poems: 1952–1988* (New Delhi: Oxford University Press, 1989), p. 224. Stanza break between lines three and four elided.

'At a certain point in history,' Chaudhuri said at the 'Against Storytelling' symposium—it can be dated to the 1980s, at the time of globalisation—'people started saying, we are born storytellers. And they said it with an air of satisfaction. One began to hear that storytelling is the primal human and communal function. That we've been telling each other stories from the beginning of time ... No, we haven't been telling each other stories from the beginning of time.'

The idea that Indian writers should tell 'our' own stories, as 'we' have always done, was, according to Chaudhuri, an invention of (literary) globalisation:

> In India 'regional' [and associated languages possess] a sort of authenticity that, say, a foreign or colonial tongue such as English doesn't. To my knowledge, the 'regional' isn't discussed in India ... in conjunction with what it has actually been inextricable from in that country—the modern, the modernist, the avant-garde, a particular intimation of strange. The perceived defeat of the regional literatures by Indian writing in English after globalization is seen, depending on which side you come from, either as a defeat of 'authentic' India, or the coming into its own ... of the postcolonial nation—but not connected, as it might be, to the retreat of avant-gardes and modernisms everywhere ... The 'regional' ... is hardly ever seen in India for what it has often been—an elite, high, counterculture project, imperiously overturning the conventions of nationalism and identity. (*Origins of Dislike*, 247)

By reducing Indian writing to personal, not to say nativist, authenticity, the imperative for stories undercuts, for Chaudhuri, the rich and complex history of West Bengal modernism, aesthetic innovation and intellectual inquiry that is foundational for his work. The mandated production of first-person stories scented with local colour for the export market undermined the validity of work stigmatised as aesthetic and difficult. Chaudhuri provides an early nineteenth-century example of this Orientalism in a riposte from Calcutta-based Anglo-Indian Henry Meredith Parker:

So the English critic complains that we are not Oriental enough, and your master begs that our lucubrations may henceforth be lighted by lamps filled with uttr; that we will compose in bowers of gul, growing green and thick under the shade of the tamarind and the pepul; that we will abstain from all food but kubaubs and pillaus; that our bread may be Bakhir Khana, and our drink sherbet of rose apples, while we tinge the web of our story with all the henna and soormah of the East.[24]

In *The Arimaspia,* Thomas McEvilley traces the classic origin of this pernicious trope to Megasthenes (fourth-century BCE Greek historian): 'I come to suspect that it is a racist projection, to the effect that dark skinned peoples can't deal with abstraction, that they are associated with the instincts, and so on.'[25]

Meanwhile, in a kind of self-colonialisation, aka blowback, the West has internalised its own supremacist imperatives for the natural and virtuous and against artifice and the cosmopolitan. The result is compulsory storytelling as shibboleth, based on sacrosanct authenticity—the *jargon of storytelling*—to adapt Max Horkheimer and Theodor Adorno's 'jargon of authenticity'. Intersectionality, which is the acknowledgment of possibly incommensurable identifications, is airbrushed into the fiction of a holistic single, seamless identity.

But, as Chaudhuri tells it, the story is more complex than that. Following Deleuze and Gramsci, we may think of the relation of major to minor, high and low, center to periphery, in terms of hegemony or mastery. Chaudhuri shows how the transvaluation of minor to major can fall into Orientalist traps of their own, while giving insight

---

[24] Parker quoted in *The Origins of Dislike*, p. 238.
[25] Thomas McEvilley, *The Arimaspia* (Kingston, NY: McPherson & Company, 2014), p. 228. Perhaps this is echoed still, albeit now valued as positive, in Yeats's ecstatic 1912 introduction to Tagore: 'The work of a supreme culture, they yet appear as grass and the rushes'; quoted in the introduction to *Name Me a Word: Indian Writers Reflect on Writing*, ed. Meena Alexander (New Haven: Yale University Press, 2018), p. xx.

into why Indian poetry in English seems formally conservative and overly Anglophilic to an American attuned to the radical modernists and the New American Poets, such as Antin, but ignorant of India. In 'Nissim Ezekiel: Poet of a Minor Literature', in *The Origins of Dislike*, he casts Ezekiel (1924–2004) as the iconic modern (post-Independence) Indian poet writing in English.[26] English in India, as Chaudhuri stresses, is marked by being the colonial language among many local tongues but also, for Ezekiel, a cosmopolitan, rather than regional, language. Ezekiel's first language was Marathi.

Ezekiel radiates double-consciousness, and in more than one way. He averts the role of the authentic storyteller who rejects European aesthetic innovation. He's local but not just local and his work engages different kinds of locality and foreignness; Chaudhuri's discussion of his work shows that such binaries are better understood as situational than as fixed, as conflicts within a poetics rather than points of policy. Ezekiel sets the stage 'In India' and in his Biblical diasporic poem, 'Lamentation':

> ... Here among the beggars,
> Hawkers, pavement sleepers,
> Hutment dwellers, slums ...
> Suffering the place and time,
> I ride my elephant of thought,
> A Cézanne slung around my neck.
>   ('In India')

> My lips lack prophesy
> My tongue speaketh no great matters

---

[26] In A. Ragu, *The Poetry of Nissim Ezekiel* (New Delhi: Atlantic Publishers, 2002), Ragu calls Ezekial 'the cultural tzar of English poetry in India' (p. 1). Ragu's study begins by signalling troubling gender politics in Ezekiel's poems and goes on to make an unconvincing case against Raj Rao's critique of Ezekial's naturalising, not to say, primitivising woman in one of his best-known poems, 'Poet, Lover, Birdwatcher', which begins 'To force the pace and never to be still / Is not the way of those who study birds / Or women. / The best poets wait for words' (Ragu, pp. 40–41). In *The Origins of Disklike*, in his discussion of the minor poet's affect, Chaudhuri cites this passage, emphasising the final line (p. 232).

> The words of the wise are wasted on me
> Fugitive am I and far from home
> A vagabond and every part of me is withered
> ('Lamentation')[27]

In his 'Very Indian Poems in English' and 'Goodbye Party for Miss Pushpa T.S.' (below), Ezekiel perverts the nativist demands made on Henry Meredith Parker:

> Friends,
> our dear sister
> is departing for foreign
> in two three days,
> and
> we are meeting today
> to wish her bon voyage.
> You are all knowing, friends,
> what sweetness is in Miss Pushpa.
> I don't mean only external sweetness
> but internal sweetness.[28]

In these ideolectical poems, Ezekiel averts mastery, turning the tables on both authentic storytelling and Orientalist condescension, while risking censure for making fun of (rather than *with*) very distinctively non-King's-English pidgin. Or is Ezekiel, like William Carlos Williams on LSD, making present in poetry the languages of the ear, creating an Indian English as distinct as Williams's American English?[29]

Chaudhuri writes about Ezekiel's work not as the truth of the subaltern but as minor poetry aware of itself, that is, as minor and as

---

[27] *Collected Poems*, pp. 132 and 72.
[28] *Collected Poems*, pp. 191–192. See Irshad Gulam Ahmed, 'Nissim Ezekiel's Critical Nationalism and the Question of Indian English' in *Indian Literature*, 53, no. 2 (2009).
[29] I discuss ideolectical poetry in two linked essays, 'The Poetics of the Americas' in *My Way: Speeches and Poems* and 'Objectivist Blues' in *Attack of the Difficult Poems*. Ezekiel dedicates a 1953 poem to Williams: 'I do not want / to write / poetry like yours / but still I / love / the way you do it', *Collected Poems*, p. 46. Williams, of course, also had an 'other' language, also a colonial one, Spanish.

accommodating; his characterisation of Ezekiel echoes 'Prufrock': 'outwardly timorous, seemingly unconfrontational, and at once "politic, cautious, and obtuse"'.[30]

'In this case of the minor poet writing in a minor tradition, there is no possibility of grand failure; there is only the inconsequentiality of decorum,' Chaudhuri says (p. 226), going on to quote an 1830 poem of Kasiprasad Ghose, one of the first Indian poets to write in English:

> To spin such verse out I'll dare.
> And please the public ear again
> With such discordant, silly strain (p. 226)

Chaudhuri admires Ezekiel for his recognition of himself as a sometimes 'comic player'—'a poet-rascal-clown', as Ezekiel describes himself, which Chaudhuri interprets as a poet who resists grandiosity with delight, and, I'd add, a welcome irony bordering on sarcasm. 'The wise survive and serve,' writes Ezekiel in 'Background, Casually'.[31] 'Here are the two aims of the minor writer and his tradition,' Chaudhuri comments, 'to not challenge, to not ask for independence or mastery, and thereby to continue to be able to write, to produce, to "survive"' (p. 234).

> My morals had declined.
> I heard of Yoga and of Zen.
> Could I, perhaps, be rabbi saint?
> The more I searched, the less I found.
>   ('Background, Casually')

What does it say that polar opposite poets, David Antin and Nissim Ezekiel, are both Jewish (Ashkenazi and Bene Israel, respectively), born just seven years apart?

—'Fugitive am I and far from home.'

---

[30] *The Origins of Dislike*, p. 228. The internal quote is from T.S. Eliot's 'The Love Song of J. Alfred Prufrock'.
[31] 'Background, Casually' in *Name Me a Word*, pp. 123–124.

I dreamed that
Fierce men had bound my feet and hands.
The later dreams were all of words.
I did not know that words betray
But let the poems come, and lost
That grip on things the worldly prize.
...
I have made my commitments now.
This is one: to stay where I am ...
In some remote and backward place.
My backward place is where I am.
              ('Background, Casually')

÷÷÷÷÷÷≥≤÷÷÷÷÷÷.³²

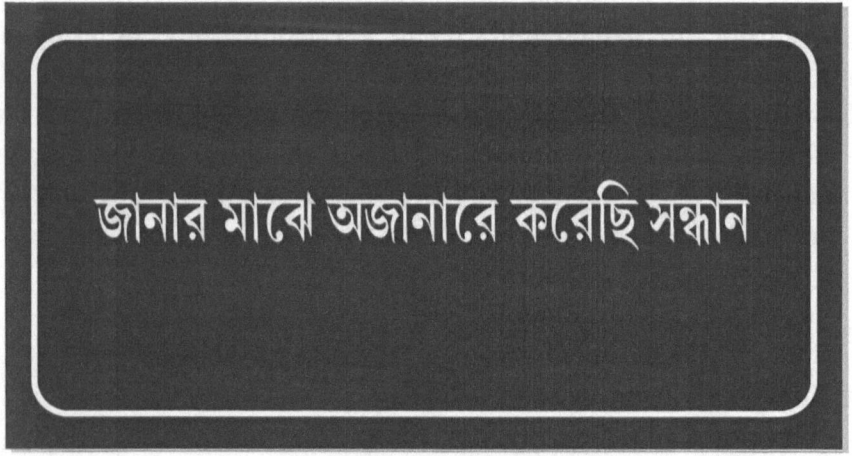

'In the midst of the known I have found the unknown',
line from a Tagore song

LXVVII.

My obituary for David Antin was printed on the inside cover of the programme for a memorial event at the Getty in Los Angeles

---

³² From Amit Chaudhuri's new 'Indian Road Signs' series, included in the catalogue to *The Sweet Shop Owners of Calcutta and Other Ideas*, an exhibition created and curated by him at the Harrington Street Arts Centre, Kolkata, in August 2018.

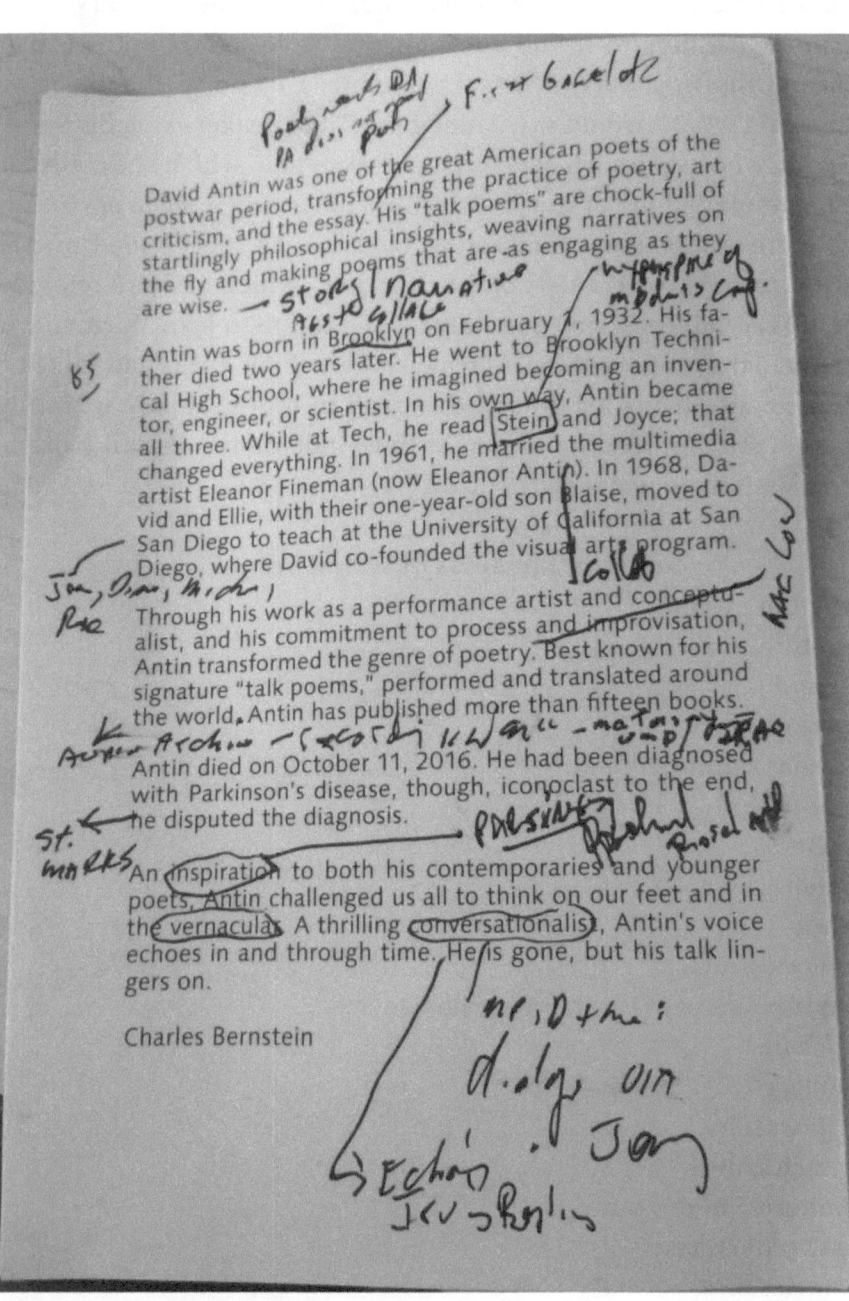

My holographic notes written in the Antin memorial programme on 4 February 2017. For my talk, I presented a commentary on my obituary, adding to it and contradicting it, based on notes I made during the first part of the programme. I came to the event not knowing what I would say. Among the first speakers was Barbara T. Smith, who asked each of us to cut a lock of hair, which she collected. This reminded me of the Jewish ritual of cutting a piece of clothing at a funeral, usually ritualised as cutting a tie. So I ended my talk with a reading of 'Rivulets of the Dead Jew', which makes a reference to this ritual. I gave my annotated programme to Jake Marmer, who immediately followed me. Marmer told us how Antin had talked to him about poems his grandfather read to him in Russian; Marmer gave a stirring reading of one of those poems in Russian (without translation, none needed).

Non-plot Elements of Verbal Art
rhythm / tempo
gesture
sound
performance
accent / timbre
allusion
echo
pitch
rime
voicelessness
audible elements of the recording device
erasure
collage
typography
rimelessness
pattern / tone / tune
patternlessness
tunelessness
haecceity
non-sensuous similarity (Benjamin, 'Doctrine of the Similar')
puns

colour
thickness
style
forms
syntax
decoration
utterance
incomprehensibility
artifice
visual organisation (line breaks, visual poetry)
context of publication
paper
digression
vocables in liberty
the word as such (not ideas but 'actual word stuff' [Williams])
the unconscious
fetish
the particular not subsumed into (reified as) story, voice, theory

∂∂∂∂.
The history of the novel is replete with works that avert the jargon of storytelling in the pursuit of narrative (in Antin's sense). There is certainly no shortage of 'story' writers who welcome multiple, competing versions, holding storytelling to an aesthetic fire. Chaudhuri will find company with Samuel R. Delany's *Motion of Light in the Water*, Lydia Davis's *End of the Story*, Raymond Federman's *Take It or Leave It*, Laura (Riding) Jackson's *Progress of Stories* and *The Telling*, Peter Straub's *The Throat*, Ko Un's *Ten Thousand Lives*, Thomas McEvilley's *The Arimsaspia*, and Paul Auster's *4321*, to name only a very few paradigmatic examples.

♣♣♣. Aversive Thinking

- Avoid frame lock, trouble consistency.
- Proliferate competing frames the way Hendrick's Gin proliferates botanicals.

- Being moody is the inability to shifts moods (to paraphrase Emerson).
- Virtue is for those who have given up on life and want to share their disapproval.

•ÅíÅë.\ÅLÅLΣΣÅ °. **More Fool You That Are Puzzled By It**
In a January 2017 conversation with reporter Mary Louise Kelly and NPR's senior vice president for news Michael Oreskes, NPR News made clear that its policy is not to use the word 'lies' when referring to blatant lying by Popular-Vote-Loser Trump and his aides. There has been much commentary on how the mediocracy contributed to the Trump election coup and this admission confirms that NPR is using a conscious strategy of doublespeak.[33]

NPR News's white-washing language abets and aids the Republican Insurgent Forces (RIF, also known as RIP), who, for their part, go on smearing anyone who opposes them as 'crooked' and liars. This is a central tactic of Operation Birther, the disinformation campaign of the RIF, aimed at using the mediocracy to broadcast their lies. In the NPR broadcast, Kelly *deceptively* used the *Oxford English Dictionary* to say that to accuse a liar of lying you need to know that they are *intending* to deceive. In the end, all of this is just NPR's refusing to accept the obvious point that it mandates the use of euphemisms for 'lie' even in the face of clear and present dangers to our democracy. The bait and switch of using 'intent' as an excuse for *euphemism* is dishonest as well as misleading.

[Kelly] says she went to the *OED* seeking the definition of 'lie'. 'A false statement made with intent to deceive,' Kelly says. 'Intent being the key word there. Without the ability to peer into Donald Trump's head, I can't tell you what his intent was. I can tell you what he said and how that squares, or doesn't, with facts.'

This implies that NPR News believes that the President of the United States might be legally insane, someone who does not know the difference between truth and lying, a pathological liar; that

---

[33] Richard Gonzales, 'NPR and the Word 'Liar': Intent Is Key', 25 January 2017, npr.org/sections/thetwo-way/2017/01/25/511503605/npr-and-the-l-word-intent-is-key.

he is delusional and may believe his own lies even though he has been repeatedly told that they are lies. This accusation is far more severe than calling the Groper-in-Chief out on his political modus operandi. If NPR News considers this plausible, they would need to say, 'Trump might be lying or he might be delusional.' Where is the psychiatric justification that allows NPR to make delusion a credible explanation for Trump's mendacity? Indeed, the quoted definition for the *OED*—noun1/1a—points out that 'falsehood' and 'untruth' are euphemisms for 'lie', not a different meaning. The quotes for this first definition of 'lie' stop in the nineteenth century. But even these belie NPR's claim:

> 1791   J. Boswell *Life Johnson* anno 1781 II. 354   Johnson had accustomed himself to use the word lie, to express a mistake or an error in relation ... though the relater did not mean to deceive.
>
> 1834   F. Marryat *Peter Simple* II. xv. 264   All lies disgrace a gentleman, white or black.
>
> 1879   J. A. Froude *Cæsar* xx. 339   It was perhaps a lie invented by political malignity.

Nor does NPR News consider *OED* definition noun/1b: 'Something grossly deceptive; an imposture.' The *OED* traces this 'transferred sense' of the word back hundreds of years. If one considers OED verb2/1a, NPR's prevaricating is brought sharp against itself: 'To utter falsehood; to speak falsely.' Boswell, again, is exemplary of the double sense: 'He lies, and he knows he lies.' (One can also say, he lies, but he does not know he lies.)

As if possessed by the ghost of logical positivist A.J. Ayer, NPR News believes that the price of objectivity is the aversion of truthfulness. Truth lies waiting, just over the bend; a lie's a thing that never ends.

A short play for NPR News:
Child steps on chair to reach cookie jar. Takes cookies out of jar and sits at kitchen table. Parental Unit walks in, stage left.
PU: I told you not to take the cookies.
C: I did not take any cookies.

PU: What is in your hands?
C: There is nothing in my hands.
PU: Don't lie to me. I can see the cookies in your hand.
C: You are the liar ... these are not cookies, they are berries.
PU: You are lying and you know it.
NPR report: PU incorrectly identifies the child's statement as a lie since PU cannot truly know what is in the child's mind. We recommend telling the child that PU has cause to question the child's statement, which appears to be inaccurate.

'He can walk fast enough when he tries, a good deal faster than I; but he can lie yet faster. He's some white operator, betwisted and painted up for a decoy. He and his friends are all humbugs,' as Melville put it in his iconic *The Confidence Man: His Masquerade*.

'More fool you that are puzzled by it.'

††† *After Thoreau and Goffman*
There are nowadays many storytellers, but it is admirable to tell because it was once admirable to live.

> I never met a person who cried "fire" when confronted by a snowball. But there are many today who cry "freedom" when confronted with tyranny. My aggrievement may be absolute to me but that does not make it greater than yours. My freedom is only that to the extent it guarantees yours. Anything different, to the extent of the difference, is not liberty; it is oppression.

783. The Unreliable Lyric

Lyric S(h)ame

~~First shun~~
then say
BEEN SHAMED
by the
~~ones whose~~
punk puns
stung your
TAME TONGUE.
Shame game
~~is a~~
vain pain:
a sucker
PUNCH *EN*
plein air.

In *Lyric Shame*, Gillian White shames those who question the jargon of authenticity in lyric poetry. White claims that active scepticism towards Romantic ideology is a form of shaming. White fights this phantom shame with her critical shaming.[34]

If story's other is narrative, what is lyric's other? 'Lyric' is so generic that it's difficult to find a term to contrast with it, unless one moves to another genre, typically 'epic'. Even so, the hegemony of a single-voice, 'scenic' lyric, the Vampiric heart of Romantic Ideology, has been contested since Blake, Byron, Swinburne, Poe, Dickinson, and the slave songs, in the nineteenth century, and Stein, Loy, Williams, Pound, Eliot, Tolson, and Riding in the early twentieth. The conventional lyric's American other in the 1930s was the 'objectivist' poem, in the 1950s 'Projective Verse' and the 'serial poem'. In the 1960s, Antin and Jerome Rothenberg suggested 'deep image' and Amiri Baraka and company, 'Black Arts'. There was a time in the early 1980s that poets

---

[34] *Lyric Shame* was published by Harvard University Press in 2014. Lytle Shaw takes the book on in 'Framing the Lyric' in *American Literary History*, 28, no. 2 (2016). My poem first appeared in *b2o*, 20 April 2017.

advocated against the scenic lyric with terms such as 'analytic lyric' or 'transcendental lyric'. Ron Silliman's 'new sentence' and Antin's 'talk poems', as with 'language-centered', specifically presented themselves against the vanilla lyric.

Not voice, voices; not craft, process; not absorption, artifice; not virtue, irreverence; not figuration, abstraction; not the standard, dialect; not regional, cosmopolitan; not normal, the strange; not emotion, sensation; not expressive, conceptual; not story, narrative; not idealism, materialism.

For binary oppositions to intensify their aesthetic engagement, and not become self-parody, it helps if they fall apart, so that you question the difference, confuse one with the other, or understand the distinctions as situational, as six is up from five but down from infinity, diction so low it's high, solipsism so radical it dissolves into pure realism.

Narrative and story are made of the same cloth, share a genre, might, paradoxically, be the same, the way a broke clock is right twice a day but always impecunious, but on a lonely night in Georgia the clock's not right any time, because the morning refuses to come. For the longest time I thought 'signified' was a crypt term for 'signified', but then I learned to tango to the music of the Pragmatics in the House of Lost Spades.

Or such is the confession of a high functioning fyslecic {dyslecic} {dusleci} [dyslexic]. There is no left or right, just degrees of left and right in relation of other points in space. [*Hey! Who are you calling a point in space!*]

To be against binary oppositions is what it's against. 'Dedualise', yes, in the sense of 'always dialecticise' and 'historicise'. Which is to say, don't neutralise conflicts in pursuit of reconciliation: the rhetorical heightening of conflict is the sine qua non of an activist poetics.

It's de rigueur for those poetry practices formally known as the avant-garde (PPFKAAG [Brit. /ˈpʌfkɔːg/, U.S. /ˈpəfˌkɔg/]) to be shamed for a lack of lyricism, emotion, humanity, even if those poetry practices reject the whole God-damn avant-garde schtick (as I done done).

Even those in the PPFKAAG hate it and there is nothing they hate more than other sectors of PPFKAAG or those whose work they most envy in their own sector.[35]

A tried and false path to transient official verse culture acceptance (TOVCA) is to attack the avant-garde for its lack of virtue (LoV) and total affect failure (TAF). *Transient* because it is unable to form a stable relationship.

Hatred of the avant-garde / opens doors / that slam / behind you.

But what do I know? I am just an unreliable lyric poet peddling tales, singing the same song all the day long.

And into the night.

‹‹‹‹‹‹‹‹‹‹‹‹‹.

XXX.

Charles Blow, who has offered the best *New York Times* commentary on Trump, notes BLT's sinister usurpation of the rage of black

---

[35] See my study *Avant-Garde Self-Hatred* (Brooklyn Free State: Hungadunga, Hungadunga, Hungadunga, and McCormack, 2018).

nationalism in the cause of white supremacism. He quotes a prescient 2015 comment by rapper Ja Rule:

> Trump is very entertaining. He speaks very openly and candidly about what he feels. I think it's a breath of fresh air for everybody to hear it. It's not always the politically correct thing, but I think that's what people are enjoying about Trump being in the running … He has always been an outspoken person. I'm not shocked by anything that comes out of his mouth at all. He's like a rapper.[36]

Trump is a master storyteller, shooting out plot elements via Twitter as if tweets were bullets in a demonic machine gun. He distracts from his own distractions: sucker punch followed by sand in the eye, then iron boot to the balls.

There is no narrative transformation to Trump's plot lines, but there is a continuing (and fraudulent) story of aggrieved authenticity, a frame that is reinforced with each tweet. No one plays aggrievement better than Trump because he understands it as a stunt, a scam, a performance, a taunt—a confidence game. Trump goes out of his way to make his lies as blatant as possible, because his lies are the guarantors—the jargon—of his authenticity. The problem with Trump is not that he is 'post-truth' or 'fake news' but that, as a storyteller, he seems more real than his most frequent detractors, albeit this is a hyperreal siren's song that is almost impossible to tune out. The storytelling is compelling, even for those who disdain it. As shipwrecks pile up on the rocky shores of the real, I remain hooked on the story feed, powerless as any junky lying on the side of the road.

If the story is believable, the facts don't matter. To be a truth teller has nothing to do with facts but with the perceived authenticity of the teller. The genuine, based on the fundamental truth of aggrievement, is the Trump card, his Dark ace in the hole.

---

[36] Charles Blow, 'Trump, 'He's "Like a Rapper"', *The New York Times*, 23 July 2018, p. A19. Paul Krugman's commentary is also exemplary.

8.

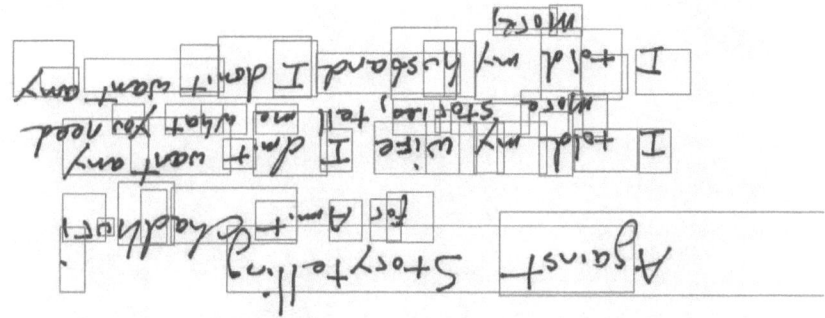

‹‹‹‹‹‹›››. *After Pound and for Shklovsky's Plotless Prose*
Never use any word that contributes to a plot.
EACH SENTENCE MUST RESIST THE SENTENCE BEFORE IT.
Even the absence of narrative had to be narrated.

ΔΔΔΔΔΔ.
'The disjointed and superfluous are what preoccupy Tagore at the end of the nineteenth century,' Chaudhuri explains. He quotes Tagore on the propensity to filter out what doesn't fit from our stories, so that 'only a small fraction' of the 'tremors' and 'comings and goings' of perception are acknowledged. 'This is chiefly because one's mind, like a fisherman, casts a net of integration and accepts only what it can gather at a single haul: everything else eludes it. [The mind] has the power to move all irrelevancies far away from the path of its set purpose.'[37]

The task of poetry is to bring the nets into view. *A task anyway …*

$\sqrt{\int} \tilde{} \mu \leq \geq \div \geq \div$. Eulogy for David Antin in English English

---

[37] 'Unconstitutional Spaces', in *The Origins of Dislike*, pp. 200–201. The Tagore passage is significant for Chaudhuri as he also cites it in the introduction to *Clearing a Space: Reflections on India, Literature and Culture* (Oxford: Peter Lang, 2008), p. 26

> if andrew motion is a poet i don't want to be a poet
> if philip larkin was a poet i don't want to be a
> poet   if david antin was a poet   i'll consider it

<small>Charles Bernstein & Nick Thurston — Eulogy for David Antin in English English — 2016</small>

Δ…÷≥≤μΩ≈√. Techniques of Erasure

'Roseland' is one of my earliest poems. It is the last poem in *Parsing* (1976). 'Roseland' samples phrases from Antin's signal talk poem, 'Sociology of Art'. It is a collage poem that erases much of Antin's talk poem, creating a network of motifs that extend and contest Antin's active thinking and his resistance to erasure. The opening page of 'Roseland' is reproduced below (from *Parsing*), followed by a compilation of the phrases I took from Antin's 'Sociology of Art'.[38] The phrases, highlighted in orange on the printed text of Antin's 'Sociology of Art', were excerpted to compose 'Roseland'. I used the excerpts mostly, but not entirely, in the order found in Antin's talk poem (for example, the first two highlighted phrases occur in the middle of 'Roseland'). I have hand-corrected a few places where I

---

[38] 'Roseland' was first published in *Parsing* (New York: Asylum's Press, 1976). A full mark-up 'Sociology of Art', together with 'Roseland', is online at http://writing.upenn.edu/epc/authors/bernstein/essays/Antin_Sociology+Roseland.pdf. Antin's talk poem was included in his 1976 collection *Talking at the Boundaries* and collected in *How Long Is the Present*.

miscopied Antin's original. All lines in 'Roseland' are taken directly from Antin's talk poem.

```
ROSELAND


                                    you need some way of
                      some set of
                         you live in a place
                                      it isn't much
                         you move out
                      you have to
                            you live at the edge
             your memory has let you down
                                   a kind of chaos
                         when you go
                                 if you face it
                      this axis this
                            the human order
                   more or less
                            you have a map
            you put yourself in position
                      and try to
                         this is the
                      a human construction
                                  you try out the space
                      try to
                            you drive on them
                 go straight
                         one might imagine
                   only grasping
                            a pity
                   a pile of rocks
```

73

something unappealing about the notion of a "primitive"
is not possible   or desirable   you use language   and in
you need some way of describing that yam   some label for
that yam   or some set of instructions by which people will find
you live in a place   and you have to get somewhere
regularly   and you have to go into places that are   confus-
ingly similar   say you live at the edge of a forest   and you
regard this as an improvement but it is clear that your memory
has let you down   since it is obvious that most hunting or for-
village   is   a human construction   is humanly devised
or arranged   even if it is a temporary station   you will have
adapted to a human order   the place that youre going into is
not humanly arranged   it is the forest   the desert   a kind of
chaos   or at least its order is "natural"   rather than "human"
when you go into it   you can become "lost"   which
means that   you cannot apprehend its order   or relate its
order to your human order   so what do you do?   you seek
its regularities   you make a map   the sun rises regularly
more or less regularly   in the east   this is the order of
nature   and it sets in the west   if you face it   the rising   try
sun   your left hand points north and your right hand south
this axis is the order of culture   the human order   now
you lay out the space   with your home at the center   or at
you mark off proportionate distances in your picture   you have
a map   now anytime you are in the forest   if you are confused   all you have to do is find out where you are in your map
to do this you look for the sun   you put yourself in position

⇑ ⁊ ⁊ §&. The Last Time I Saw David was on 4 December 2014

Ellie and David were going to come to dinner the day after David's Poetry Project talk, for which I had made a video that is on PennSound. In the Parish Hall at St. Mark's, David laid himself bare, turning the talk poem onto his physical movement in the space, as he walked away from the podium to show us, as if he were Yvonne Rainer, the way his Parkinson's debilitated his bearing. In the talk poem, almost David's last, he pushed hard against the Parkinson's diagnosis. His thought and his body were one and yet at odds with

each other. Antin was making present an experiential dimension that defied intelligibly, being there, in that space, as fully present as any poet can be, standing alone before an audience. No, not alone. *Next to us.*
The following morning David called me. He spoke in a whisper.
He said he couldn't come to dinner.
That he was no longer able to speak.
That he had lost his voice.
~~~~~~~~~~~~

Charles Bernstein and David Antin.
Photo © Alan Thomas. 15 May 2011.

'What Difference Does It Make?'
For and Against Storytelling via the Novels of Kiran Nagarkar

Anjum Hasan

Kiran Nagarkar's 1974 novel *Saat Sakkam Trechalis—Seven Sixes Are Forty-Three* in the English translation—is a modernist collage: fragmentary, dream-like, sidestepping linearity and conclusiveness, its hero repeatedly coming up against the absurdity of middle-class life, religious belief, childhood terrors and, most recurrently, romantic love. The novel describes the interior landscape of a dissolute and moneyless young man in Bombay and Pune of the 1960s and 1970s. Kushank Purandare loves women, one after the other or simultaneously, but the novel is not a love story: he cannot submit erotic feelings to conventions such as monogamy or ideals of permanence and responsibility. And so the refrain of one of his lovers—'What difference does it make?'—becomes a theme of the novel.

After this novel, his first, Nagarkar would not publish another book till two decades later when the novel *Ravan and Eddie* appeared. The place of *Seven Sixes Are Forty-Three* in Nagarkar's oeuvre has usually been discussed in terms of language—he wrote this first novel in Marathi and then went on to write several more in English. And that move is seen as proof of his linguistic talents. Stylistically *Seven Sixes Are Forty-Three* was considered unprecedented. One wag asked, on hearing that it was going to be translated into English, 'But should it not be translated into Marathi first?' and its discontinuous structure apparently befuddled early readers.

But what the focus on Marathi versus English obscures is how far Nagarkar also shifted from that restrained, jagged, rhetorical style of his debut to create the chatty if not voluble voice he used in *Ravan and Eddie*. In the latter he seems to laugh off the searing angst that saturates *Seven Sixes Are Forty-Three* to focus instead on the resilient, sometimes even joyful, pragmatism of the poor. It could also be that the India of the early 1990s in which he was writing this second novel was no longer the country in which a Kushank Purandare might convincingly essay his brooding lyricism. *Ravan and Eddie* is set earlier in time—from the mid-1940s to the early 1960s—but in tone it could be described as an Indian English novel of the 1990s—exuberant, larger than life and indubitably filmi in the resolve of its down-and-out characters to overcome life's challenges. Other similarly effervescent novels from the same period that come to mind are I. Allan Sealy's *Trotter Nama*, Shashi Tharoor's *Great Indian Novel*, Mukul Kesavan's *Looking Through Glass* and, of course, the fiction of Salman Rushdie.

Just two years after *Ravan and Eddie*, Nagarkar published a third novel called *Cuckold* and with this—a 600-page saga set in sixteenth-century Rajasthan—he seemed to have reinvented himself all over again. If *Seven Sixes Are Forty-Three* is remarkable for the naked, bitter gaze of its hero on all of life, and for Nagarkar's subversion of the conventions of the realist novel, and *Ravan and Eddie* for how cramped communal Bombay life, however desperate, can be rendered a poignantly funny thing, then *Cuckold* compels for its sustained attention on the inner life of a medieval prince in a register that is sombre, richly descriptive and replete with the most finessed emotional nuances.

The prince, the Maharaj Kumar, speaks to us, mostly in first person, in a contemporary English idiom that makes surprisingly immediate the complex political life of the kingdom of Mewar as well as his tortured relationship with his wife Mira—who would go on to become the popular poet-saint, Mirabai, a figure who has generally been thought of in mythical rather than historical terms. In *Cuckold*, there is none of the first novel's doubt about the significance and purpose of human action and none of the second novel's eulogising of working-class heroes. Instead, the focus has shifted to a consideration of the yawning gap between the public and the private, convention and desire, politics and love.

I will come back to these three novels which seem to have nothing in common, and I will explore Nagarkar's relationship to storytelling and its opposite via a slightly closer reading of all three books. But before that, I want to ask what storytelling generally means today in relation to literature. There are two possibly related but not always well-argued-for anathemas that have given storytelling its contemporary appeal because it is meant to suggest an escape from them—one is the sin of boring people, the other the shibboleth of cultural elitism.

———

In 2015, I was speaking on a panel at a literary festival with the novelists Manu Joseph and Zia Rahman Haider. The theme was the literary novel which Joseph, who more or less hijacked the discussion, unilaterally declared alienating to readers. He did not provide examples but from his comments one inferred that this beast was the sort that won awards, sold poorly and lacked a plot, and whose authors were persistent apologists for unreadability. That his own novel, *Serious Men*, had won a leading award not too long ago *and* sold well enough for him to make, he said, a living from it, did not seem to interfere with the argument. Despite his vituperation, Joseph's point seemed to be a simple and banal one—that is, the market decides what is worthwhile fiction and everything else be damned.

Joseph has, before and since, touched publicly on this point, so I will use him as an example here of an attitude which—in being held by a practitioner of a genre he considers largely worthless—seems self-defeating. And yet it is not considered strange. Joseph's views are seen as either worth agreeing with or important to dismiss but not paradoxical. Zia Rahman Haider did the latter during our discussion by upholding his right to cultivate his chosen aesthetic as a writer, even if this is not rewarded by the market. But rarely is it noticed that arguments such as Joseph's imply a curious solipsism; they are an echo chamber in which each writer creates for himself the version of the novel he has authorised.

It is not uncommon to come upon other Indian English writers actively resisting the very idea of Indian English writing as something effete, second-hand, or just plain inauthentic. This embarrassment with the category seems to have become intrinsic to it. For his part, Manu Joseph scoffs at the creators of so-called high literature, and his charge is that this high-mindedness is a cover for mediocrity. Such robust writers as have their ears to the ground know the value of storytelling for the masses, whereas only wishy-washy liberals disregard storytelling in the books they write mainly for mutual approbation. In an interview with a newspaper, Joseph later said, 'I have a grouse about what is considered serious literature. The way activists have created a reward system for unreadable novels is a crime against art. So when social frailties are sold in the form of novels, which don't have any stories or anything—that irritates me.'

Probing Joseph's views further, one finds that he equates moral seriousness in art with ideological obduracy. He has written against activism in art—the move to replace what is entertaining and interesting with what is merely empathetic to all points of view. There is certainly, here in India and elsewhere, a growing conformism regarding who to represent and how—and an ever-ready willingness to take offence on behalf of one or another cultural identity. (Joseph's first novel, *Serious Men*, a hilarious account of the brilliant conniving of a Dalit man to secure a place in the sun for his child, was read by some as showing the underclasses and women in a poor light, even though it moves away from the victim narrative usually associated with Dalit lives to present, in strikingly aphoristic prose, a bracing anger.) But Joseph does not distinguish such policing of literature with what is, or at least once was, a liberal catholicity.

Why then this wilful neglect of the modern capabilities of liberalism? In the interview quoted above, Joseph points out that except as some lowly derivatives of the West, as Indians 'we don't know what we are when we're modern'. This is not an estrangement of the kind that Kushank Purandare is subject to in *Seven Sixes Are Forty-three*, but a rejection of something like an Indian sensibility.

Joseph's next novel, *Miss Laila, Armed and Dangerous*, while shaped like a thriller and so, naturally, replete with storytelling, is also aimed at ridiculing both liberal 'eggheads' and hardened right-wingers. This is at best only mildly amusing; it is also indicative of where Joseph thinks storytelling can take us—if nothing has value then the only role left to entertainment is to take down everything.

To valorise storytelling, then, is to hope something exists in literature that could distract us from our own emptiness. For such valorisation not just shuns that 'activist' taking of hard lines, it apparently also shuns the opposite—open-endedness, ambivalence, nuance, ennui, what Joseph calls 'social frailties'. The discomfort with oneself as a Westernised India, the fear of boredom, the alienation from the dominant currents of political opinion, and the belief in the ultimate justice of the free market—all these seem to come together in the propagation of storytelling, which now means much more than just the folksy longing for a beginning, middle and end.

To reject one's modernity as Joseph does is a sentiment interestingly incongruous with *Seven Sixes Are Forty-Three*, even though, in the way that its main character tries to forge meaning out of his relationships and his run-ins with poverty and cruelty, this novel is a search for a modern identity. What makes the search compelling is that it is not foreclosed by any of the available formulations regarding what is or is not Indian. Nagarkar—or his character Purandare—is truly fascinated by just the human condition while also completely absorbed in day-to-day local reality. Early in the novel Purandare says to the 'you' he is often addressing—one or the other of the various women he has loved and left:

> You see people. In groups, in countries, in societies. Indians, Englishmen, Spaniards, Germans, Chinese. And then Caucasians, Semites, Mongolians [...] Perhaps your training as a sociologist has something to do with that. I see only human beings. As individuals. Isolated, occasionally in groups. [...] At best, I am a practising human being. Nothing else. I don't understand the Indian subcontinent, it doesn't exist for me, it doesn't worry me.

His reading—and these names are scattered like clues through the book—seems to consist largely of European modernists such as Haldor Laxness, Elias Canetti, Pär Lagerqvist, Jean Anouilh and Albert Camus. (And in some ways he is a completer nihilist than that better-known nihilist, Camus's Meursault. Unlike *The Outsider* which, despite its hero's anti-establishment outlook, follows the novelistic conventions of set-up, climax and denouement, there is no single crucial incident in *Seven Sixes Are Forty-Three*. Nothing in the novel has more or less significance than anything else, just as nothing in Purandare's existence does. Yet this does not make him more passive or indifferent than Meursault. In fact, he experiences other people's suffering more deeply than the unfeeling Algerian ever could.)

Purandare reads these writers matter-of-factly, not as an Indian trying to internalise the West; they seem as inherent to his environment as Hindustani classical music or the films of Satyajit Ray. If Manu Joseph is able to hold forth on literature without ever talking about actual books—literature as a series of positions rather than a history of texts—then Nagarkar shows the opposite tendency here in his interest in literature as experience rather than argument. But nothing in this experience is in the nature of an event. If storytelling hinges on events, here we have a novel about incidents, and the seeming randomness of those that life throws up. 'It frightens me ... to think what small and irrelevant things change the flow of our lives,' he says.

When read against other modernist landmarks from the same era, featuring similarly introspective, dissatisfied heroes, such as U.R. Ananthamurthy's *Bharathipura*, Vinod Kumar Shukla's *The Servant's Shirt* or O.V. Vijayan's *Legends of Khasak*, one realises that Nagarkar's aim is not so much posing a central moral question to do with individual purpose and dignity in a largely hostile society as playing with fictional form to question life itself.

Nagarkar's second novel, *Ravan and Eddie*, however, begins with an event, a child's birth, and on the night of independent India's first Christmas Eve, so we can't help but wonder what it might owe to that other, older 'midnight' novel. But it appears that this date has no special significance for Nagarkar. While Salman Rushdie's hero in *Midnight's Children*, Saleem Sinai, is born 'mysteriously handcuffed to history' precisely because he is born just as India is freed from the Raj, in the case of *Ravan and Eddie*, 1947 is little more than a chronological marker and the departure of the British makes no noticeable difference to the folk in one of Bombay's colonial-era tenements, the Central Works Department Chawl.

Further, even though, like Sinai, Eddie is born in melodramatic circumstances (as his father's corpse is being borne to the cemetery and before his mother can get to hospital), these two narratives are markedly different in one other respect. The mythmaking in *Midnight's Children* is driven by the author's project of merging history with personal destiny, while in *Ravan and Eddie*, the myths emerge from within the imagination of the two children. Saleem Sinai may delight for other reasons but he is never really allowed a child's psychology, whereas Ravan and Eddie slowly stumble up before our eyes. Nagarkar's ability to speak and feel from within the minds of his child characters is brilliantly illustrated by the legend of Ravan, the murderer.

As a bubbly one-year-old, Ravan leaps out of his mother's arms and flies straight from the balcony of the chawl's fourth floor into the arms of aircraft mechanic Victor Coutinho down below. Ravan survives but Victor dies from the shock of the impact. His wife, Violet, spends the next couple of decades in grim mourning, and their two children, Eddie and Pieta, grow up fatherless and poor. Close neighbours Ravan and Eddie are thus expected to be enemies. The fact that Ravan as an infant in some sense 'killed' Eddie's father is revealed to him only when he is ten years old. A little earlier, in a scene unrelated to this great revelation, he tries to persuade his friend Chandrakant Dixit to join the revivalist Hindu Sabha. Hearing him try to lure his son, Ravan is shouted out of the Dixit house by Chandrakant's father.

Sala, you bloody murderers of Mahatma Gandhi, yes, yes, you, don't pretend to be so surprised, you murdered the Mahatma, you have the gall to come to my house and preach the gospel of the Sabha.

When he is later told he also did away with Eddie Coutinho's father, he acquiesces though he has no memory of either of these events. Ravan will acquire fame among his peers as a murderer of both Gandhi and Victor Coutinho and this fame will occasionally become a source of power for the boy. Yet it will cloud his life and dog him till his adult years—a misunderstanding of childhood that has hardened into fate.

Ravan and Eddie nevertheless end up becoming friends because both resolutely believe they are destined to be famous showmen. Imagining personal success in terms of success in Bombay's show business is as crucial to this novel and its sequel *The Extras*, as making it in, say, Charles Dickens's early industrial London involved triumphing over impecunious origins and avaricious capitalists and becoming a 'gentleman'.

This hope that films hold out—at least the Hindi films of the 1950s and 1960s—is a humanist one: the underdog will win, not just despite his rough beginnings but also regardless of his cultural identity. Ravan and Eddie are Hindu and Christian, so the furniture of their worlds, as it were, is different, but this difference does not script their fates. This is in interesting contrast to a latter-day Bombay chawl novel—Joseph's *Serious Men*—where almost everything that his anti-hero Ayyan Mani says and does hinges on his being Dalit. Nagarkar belongs to what Manu Joseph calls Empathy Incorporated, but this empathy is less sentimental compassion for the poor, more an expression of the same humanism that in his first novel takes the form of a youthful despair at societal injustices and conventions, and which, in *Ravan and Eddie*, makes joy rather than anger the key emotion.

Both these novels then are expressions of what has been called Bombay Modern. There is, palpably, the same modernist fascination for the immediate and the quotidian evident in, say, the poems of Nagarkar's long-time friend and colleague in advertising, Arun

Kolatkar. One is inclined to describe Nagarkar as a Bombay Modern rather than a Marathi one, not just because he is bilingual but also for his disavowal of an identity connected with any one language or ethnicity. He is also a Bombay Modern in his urge to make the past contemporary, to test its accessibility to us. This is what drives his third novel, *Cuckold*. He draws this medieval history near through what he calls 'an easy colloquial currency of language'. The characters in this novel curse with words like 'damn' and think in terms of adages like 'Nero fiddled while Rome burned'. And as much as the historical particulars are clearly evoked, this is no costume drama or period piece.

Such contemporaneity does two things. It gives us a sense of the crown prince or Maharaj Kumar—the figure at the centre of the drama—from the inside as a passionately preoccupied figure, bedevilled by doubts, intelligent, sensuous and lonely. And it brings alive the dynamism of the period being described. The Kumar, even as he is trying to rein in his Krishna-besotted wife and win wars for Mewar, is engrossed in questions to do with the foolishly anachronistic aspects of Rajput chivalry. He is a man of the moment and this is not a timeless kingdom of yore but one caught in a many-pronged conflict featuring older Muslim rulers in north India, such as the Khiljis and the Lodis, the first Mughal, Babur, and the several other neighbouring Hindu states.

The situation seems to call for not just new ways of fighting wars but also new definitions of the self. In an epiphanic passage, the prince talks of how he had gods for heroes as a child but when he grew up he realised the gods are implacable. 'Their lives were turbulent but the quality of their experience rarely warped, bent or changed the way they looked at things. Their minds were impervious. Little, if anything, seeped in.'

And that is the critical contrast: the ever shifting circumstances of the mortals versus the timeless nature of the gods. Perry Anderson, in that well-known *London Review of Books* essay on historical fiction, described Giuseppe Lampedusa's 1960 novel *The Leopard* as 'the greatest historical novel of the century' for its interlocking, rare for the genre, of the historical and existentialist registers. *Cuckold* manages to do the same—it is an existential novel about life as a Rajput prince in the 1500s or, conversely, a historical novel about the sorrow of being in an incompatible marriage and living in an unsympathetic realm. In an interview Nagarkar said that after he finished the novel, he remembers telling his partner that everything in it was true. (This is interesting to consider alongside his remark, in the afterword to the novel, that 'The last thing I wanted to do was write a novel of historical veracity.') He goes on to say in the interview that by 'true' he means he was striving not for historical but 'artistic authenticity'.

What could that imply in relation to an epic work of storytelling? Moving beyond both event and incident, I want to go back to a word I used a little earlier—situation. The situation, in *Cuckold* and in Nagarkar's other novels, is the human one. Nagarkar's experiments with different forms and styles in these three novels—and his ability to incorporate so many accents—is evidence of writerly virtuosity but it also suggests a restless search for the perfect vehicle to express this artistic authenticity in the cause of his humanism. If the propagation of storytelling furthers the myth that everyone is potentially a storyteller, and so literature is indistinguishable from life, then Nagarkar shows how much art must be brought to bear on the question of which stories are worth telling.

But if the novel's art is considered a way of thinking of moral problems practically, through narrative, then Kiran Nagarkar *does* tell stories. I am drawing on Susan Sontag here, who in her essay, 'At the Same Time', discusses how the delineation of borders in the novel, its essentially circumscribed structure, its inevitable setting in a particular time and space, subverts that bizarre reality engendered by globalised media of a constant now and an always here. And this is what distinguishes literature from the stories the media tells:

> By presenting us with a limitless number of non-stopped stories, the narratives which the media relate—the consumption of which has so dramatically cut into the time the educated public once devoted to reading—offer a lesson in amorality and detachment that is antithetical to the one embodied by the enterprise of the novel.

Here then is an argument for storytelling, which is that its ethics consists in taking responsibility for selection and providing insight through closure or completion. Sontag rejects the 'spurious cultural geography of a borderless world', and Kiran Nagarkar in being at once a storyteller and against storytelling is able to make the worlds of his novels both scrupulously particular and widely resonant.

I Don't Have Wings: Vinod Kumar Shukla

Arvind Krishna Mehrotra

In one of his poems, the Hindi writer Vinod Kumar Shukla compares the flight of a bird to that of a butterfly:

> Do birds sitting on the ground
> feel that they've left the earth
> and are flying above it
> when they climb the air?
> To fly above it,
> you really have to go high.
>
> And when they return
> and sit on trees,
> do birds feel
> that it's the earth they're sitting on?
>
> I don't have wings.
>
> There's a small yellow butterfly
> flying above the earth.

If the poem can be read as a metaphor for two kinds of writer, the bird writer and the butterfly writer, then Shukla clearly belongs to the latter species. The bird in Shukla's poem doesn't know what it is distant or cut off from, or what it is returning to. Shukla's vision, by contrast, operates at ground level. The people he observes and writes about are the kind who, when they step out of the house, carry with them a tattered shopping bag, into which go the haggled down vegetables they buy. An early poem of his, from 1960, is about just this:

> A street in the bazaar,
> a busy shopper,
> carrying a soiled, frayed
> bag in each hand, one empty,
> the other full. In it,
> potatoes, leafy vegetables,
> a packet of garam masala,
> and chillies,
> both red and green.
> How I wish I'd been
> a ten rupee note
> and sheltered in that bag.
> But I was stuck
> inside my own.

These busy shoppers are modest people, and Shukla is a modest storyteller. Making do with very little, or rather making with very little, he uses materials that are of the simplest: a man, a bicycle, the falling leaf of a neem tree, dry and yellow and brittle, yet substantial enough to bear the weight of narrative. I say weight, though what I want to suggest is lightness. 'I have tried to remove weight,' said Calvino in the first of his *Six Memos for the Next Millennium*, 'sometimes from people, sometimes from heavenly bodies, sometimes from cities; above all I have tried to remove weight from the structure of stories and from language.' We could say the same about Shukla's work, both his poetry and fiction.

The Burden *(1963)*

He'd had his breakfast and was back home. No sooner was he back than he changed into his office clothes and put on his shoes. He oiled and combed his hair. He picked up the bicycle keys and the lock to put on the door. The cycle was on the veranda, from where he wheeled it out and started for office. This was his daily routine; he went through it without thinking about it twice.

He was going at a good speed even though he had plenty of time. The road ran along Phoolbagh. It took him roughly twenty minutes to reach his office. It was summer and the dry leaves of the neem trees that lined either side of the road were constantly falling. One of the leaves got lodged in his pocket. He found this odd. He continued to pedal, and as he did so he put his left hand in the pocket and tried to take out the leaf, but it crumbled and stuck to the cloth. He stopped the bike and turned out the pocket to clean it. The leaf fragments in his pocket could hardly be called heavy nor did he have to stop to remove them, but he did stop.

He had reached Phoolbagh when it struck him that he might have forgotten to lock his room. He tried hard to remember but a nagging doubt still remained. Yesterday the same thing had happened. He'd come halfway when he had to turn back. He wanted to make sure the lock was secure. He pulled at it and found that it was. Having made certain, he went to office with an easy mind.

He'd been paid two days ago. He had just one bed in his room and a trunk that he never locked, though he often thought he should get one for it. He had kept his salary in the trunk, inside the pocket of a freshly washed shirt. He'd then placed a handkerchief over the pocket to keep the money from falling out if the clothes were moved around. Perhaps he also thought that the handkerchief would conceal the money, make it less noticeable.

He lived in a rented room behind Lashkar Hotel. Bhagwat, who worked for the hotel, would come round to sweep the rooms, starting with the ones on the left. He didn't think twice before entering a room even if no one was there. Several times it happened that Bhagwat had come to sweep the room while he was bathing in the common facility. He'd hurried through the bath and returned quickly to the room. He didn't want Bhagwat to be there in his absence. He didn't trust these hotel employees one bit, though so far he'd had no complaints.

He thought he had probably locked his room, but what if he hadn't? He felt annoyed with himself for being unsure. He could still go back and check. This time he felt certain that he'd forgotten to lock it. His entire salary was in the trunk and he did not want to take a chance. If he went back, the extra pedalling might tire him out but at least the money would be safe. In any case, he was early for office. Even if he went back to the room to make sure, he wouldn't be late. Should he or should he not, he asked himself. Without being aware of what he was doing, he slowed down. He went round the traffic island, at the same slow speed, and then, pedalling furiously, returned to his room. He almost collided with a handcart loaded with a slab of ice but he managed to avoid it at the last minute.

He saw Bhagwat standing on the veranda as he approached the hotel. He didn't like this at all. He locked the bike and went up to his room. From the expression on his face and by his walk, he wanted to convey to Bhagwat that he was in a hurry and had forgotten something. While climbing the stairs he turned round to look. Bhagwat was watching him. Oh shit! Hope the bastard hasn't caught on, he thought. On reaching the room he paused and looked behind him again. Bhagwat wasn't there. He pulled at the lock and found that it was fastened. He came down whistling and there was a bounce in his step. He asked the pandit who was the hotel cook for a glass of water and then for another; he was thirsty. He left for office after drinking two glasses of water.

He felt light-hearted. He stopped the bike at a restaurant that he passed and looked at the clock on the wall. It was not yet eleven; he still had plenty of time. He'd been wise, he thought, to go back to his room and reassure himself about the lock. If he hadn't, he'd have been thinking about it all the time he was at work. These things do happen. After all, anyone can make a mistake, and the same mistake can be repeated. He could have lost the hundred and fifty rupees, his entire salary. How then would he have paid last month's bills and met this month's expenses? He may even have had to give up his room. He'd done the right thing, he told himself.

In fact, what he had feared had happened once before. The lock he had at the time was a press lock. He'd gone out for a stroll in the evening, and when he returned half an hour later he found the lock hanging open. He'd forgotten to press the shank. It had got him worried but his things were safe.

He worked with a relaxed mind and came home in the evening. He unlocked the door. He was extremely tired. The moment he lay down he felt sleepy. He closed his eyes and turned over on his side. It felt good to stretch his arms and legs. His daily round to the office and back required a lot of cycling and his legs felt heavy, as though he'd climbed several flights of stairs to reach his room. After a while he got up and opened the trunk. He took out all the money that was in the shirt pocket and went down to pay off his debts. He paid for the previous month's food and the rent. Then he handed Bhagwat a fiver to give to the dhobi. He was out of oil, soap and toothpaste, which he bought from the corner shop. He possessed two handkerchiefs and purchased another. For the past month he'd been wondering if he should buy two more banians and this time he thought he would. He only had the one pair of shoes and needed to buy chappals, but with only eight rupees and a few annas left to last him the whole month, he decided not to. He'd have bought them if he had some more money. He carried the stuff back to his room.

The next morning, before setting out for office, he wore his new banian, changed the set of clothes he was wearing. In his pocket was the new handkerchief. He combed his hair and put on his shoes, then picked up the bicycle keys and the lock.

He'd only gone a short distance when the faint misgiving obscurely entered his mind that he'd forgotten to lock the room. He smiled and shook his head, then continued to go along at the same speed. If someone had then seen him smiling to himself they'd have been surprised. There were neem trees on either side of the road. It was summer and hundreds of dry leaves were falling, but not one of them swirled down and found its way into his pocket. He carried on cycling, without stopping or slowing down.

The leaf did not find its way into the man's pocket, but we know where Shukla found his story. He found it in a moment we are all familiar with: it's when we realise that we may have left something unlocked (a house, a car, a piece of luggage), or left something on, like the gas burner. Once we have made sure that the house is locked, the burner turned off, we don't think of it again. It's this dead, unbreathing moment that Shukla revives, before edging it away. 'He carried on cycling, without stopping or slowing down.' You begin to wonder if you are ever alive except when you discover yourself in the pages of a book.

Anxiety is followed by a sense of relief. When he finds that the lock is fastened and his fear was unfounded, the man comes 'down whistling and there [is] a bounce in his step'. At one point, a little earlier in the story, he covers the money in the shirt pocket with a handkerchief. This is something that a coyote or a woodpecker, creatures that hide their food cache, would have recognised. It's an act as avian or animal as it is human. We all hide our purses, our house keys and even, if there are predatory servants around, our food.

Shukla's storytelling turns on small everyday acts. Often on the things that flicker and vanish in the mind's peripheral vision before we can quite see them. This is what poems also do: they try and grasp a disappearing thought or impression and bring it into hard focus. As the title poem of Shukla's first full-length collection has it, 'That man put on a new woollen coat and went away like a thought':

> That man put on a new woollen coat and went away like a thought.
> In rubber flip-flops I struggled behind.
> The time was six in the morning, the time of being undressed—it was freezing cold.
> Six in the morning was like six in the morning.
> There was a man standing under a tree.
> In the mist it looked like he was standing inside his own blurred shape.
> The blurred tree looked exactly like a tree.
> To its right was a blurred horse of inferior stock,
> looking like a horse of inferior stock.
> The horse was hungry, the mist like a grassy field to him.

> There were other houses, trees, roads, but no other horse.
> There was only one horse. I wasn't that horse,
> but my breath when I panted was indistinguishable from the mist.
> If the man standing at that one spot under the tree was the boss,
> then to him I was a horse at a gallop, horseshoes nailed to my boot soles.

While diverting our attention with metaphor and linguistic play ('Six in the morning was like six in the morning'), Shukla surreptitiously introduces his moral vision. The play is deadly serious. We recall Calvino's idea of lightness, where lightness does not mean lightweight. 'There was only one horse. I wasn't that horse', protests the speaker of the poem, the man in rubber flip flops. But in the eyes of the boss, he is 'a horse at a gallop, horseshoes nailed to [his] boot soles'. The working man has changed places with the workhorse. The boss remains what he is, an unattainable idea of wealth, someone snug in the woollen coat of his thoughts. Shukla, in the poem, identifies with the man in flip flops, just as he does with the man who lacks money to buy, after meeting the month's expenses, a new pair of chappals. To change the butterfly metaphor, Shukla could be described in similar terms, the writer in cheap footwear. Against storytelling segues into against writing, against a certain idea of writing, of writer.

At the Jaipur Literature Festival 2011, Vinod Kumar Shukla asked Sara Rai why so many people were standing in line, each clutching a book. Told that they were all waiting to have their books signed by J.M. Coetzee, he looked puzzled. Hindi writers sign books, but privately, and seldom is there a line of people waiting for them to do so. Moreover, the name Coetzee meant nothing to him, nor did the names of the other world writers present on the occasion. And this despite the fact that his own books have been translated into French,

Italian, and English. One explanation for it could be that he reads only in Hindi, which perhaps has more speakers than Mandarin Chinese but in which little gets translated. Even if it were, you doubt whether Shukla would be interested. Recently, when asked in an email if he was familiar with any European writers, for it is they who often come to mind when you read him, Shukla did not evade the question. He simply ignored it. The question did not deserve an answer.

'There is nothing of me except what is here,' Shukla says in one poem. Shukla's 'here' is a specific place, Raipur and, before that, Rajnandgaon, both cities in the tribal belt of India. Rajnandgaon is where he was born in 1937 into a family of Saryuparin Brahmins who hailed from Uttar Pradesh, and Raipur is where he taught agricultural extension at the Indira Gandhi Agricultural University. It meant travelling to the surrounding villages and acquainting farmers with new agricultural techniques. He retired as associate professor in 1996. This is not your usual trajectory of a great writer, but therein lies the paradox of Vinod Kumar Shukla.

Though there was until the 1960s little to distinguish Rajnandgaon and Raipur from the other wayside stations on the Howrah–Bombay rail line, in Shukla's eyes they encompass the known world. Were it left to him, he would still be living in the house of his childhood that he writes about in his autobiographical essay 'Old Veranda':

> Ours was a family of four brothers living under one roof. The roof's shadow belonged to my youngest uncle, who was called Chachaji. He was called this at home and also outside, but wherever he was he largely kept to himself. Everyone was in awe of him. If he stepped out of the house more than he usually did, he came up against the world as if against a wall. He came up against it even when he was at home.
>
> As happens in joint families, there would be quarrels. Guns would come out but were never fired. The women never quarrelled. Perhaps this was because of Amma, who continued to work quietly despite the chaos of marriages, births, and deaths. I don't know how, but her quiet would have a calming effect on those who were grieving, and those who were full of joy would find the space around them expand to accommodate their laughter.

Amma would be up when it was still dark and would be the last to sleep. You could hear her in the kitchen putting things away, the clattering sounds like a lullaby for the night, sending it to sleep. Even the plants listened to her. As soon as it was twilight, the guava, the drumstick tree, and the tulsi in the courtyard would doze off, as would the soft grass in the corner and the two tomato plants that had appeared on the rubbish heap. The tall peepul tree to the east of the house would look in, and seeing the other plants asleep, go to sleep itself.

If she saw an ant in the fire crawling on a dung-cake she would pull out the dung-cake and save the ant. In the same way, she would save us from small everyday fires and hope that they wouldn't recur. The burn on her hand would not have healed before she burned herself again. Her daily routine was like a thread going through the different things she did, stringing them together. She never felt the needle's prick, but I did. In the papers I read about a man who was hospitalised and discovered to have hundreds of needles in his body. Was my condition similar to that man's?

The large family living under 'one roof' is an idea that he returns to also in a poem. By the time the poem ends, though, the family has become the human family, and the 'one roof' is not of a house in Rajnandgaon but the sky. A particular childhood memory has here opened out into a feeling that is not dissimilar to what W.H. Auden called a 'vision of Agape', a vision of shared unerotic love. Going a step further, Shukla shares the feeling with all of creation, including the earth:

Would that we all had lived together
under one roof
without separate kitchens—
grandfather, great aunt,
father, uncle, siblings—
and stayed in the same neighbourhood.
Nature lives beside nature,
grass next to grass,
mud next to mud,

and in the wind live
storms, hurricanes,
and scent-laden gusts.
Without knots,
there's one wind circling the earth,
together with our breathing.

Shukla, who seldom travels and has been outside India perhaps only three or four times on literary junkets, would agree with Hazlitt that 'Foreign travel especially makes men pedants, not artists. What we seek, we must find at home or nowhere'.

Shukla must be among the few writers alive whose work has appeared in journals and anthologies where world literature is published or discussed—*Granta, Modern Poetry in Translation, Some Kind of Beautiful Signal, The Baffler, n+1*—but who has heard neither of these journals nor of world lit. In contrast to his unawareness of the term and his indifference to the subjects that keep the assembly line of global fiction moving (historical trauma, acts of terrorism, personal turmoil) is the attention he lavishes on the fleeting observations, thoughts, memories, and gestures that for most of us, regardless of where we live, constitute our lives. To read him is to read not a fictionalised version of what is already known, but what is constantly being inscribed in and erased from the margins of our consciousness.

'The Burden' and 'Old Veranda' are quoted from *Blue Is Like Blue: Stories* by Vinod Kumar Shukla, trans. Arvind Krishna Mehrotra and Sara Rai (HarperCollins, 2019). Reprinted with permission.

A Story in Memory of John Ashbery

Geoffrey O'Brien

All life
Is as a tale told to one in a dream
In tones never totally audible
Or understandable, and one wakes
Wishing to hear more,

John Ashbery, 'Litany'

1

I don't remember where I heard this story.
After the cessation of hostilities
in the Second World War
an American soldier
waiting with so many others to go home
sat cross-legged on the hot deck of a troop ship
reading a paperbound mystery novel—
it might have been *The Camera Clue*
or *The Fatal Kiss* or *The X-Ray Murders*—
and as he came to the end of every second page
he tore that leaf from the book
and passed it to the soldier on his left,
each leaf in turn passed thus
from hand to hand around the deck
until the whole book was read
by hundreds of soldiers with nothing else to do
but measure the time as it leaked away,

so that the cheap little paperback—
it might have been *Reno Rendezvous*
or *Holiday Homicide* or *The Doctor Died at Dusk*—
acquired precious value as one soldier at a time
found a temporary home in some random wad
of narrative padding or incidental description,
some flirty come-on or slangy comeback,
freezing it in place as if by the hypnotic ray
in a comic book, even as the soldier on his left
nudged him to read faster, the way, after all,
the author must have intended, since mysteries are designed
to make time pass as quickly and imperceptibly
as possible, to obliterate time and replace it
with what is experienced as endless and endlessly
pleasurable, even while despite the impulse
to slow down and savour the lovely stillness
of an immobilised sentence the soldier felt driven
to get to the end of it, and if the light held
the last reader on deck would have been left
with a now useless pile of unbound pages,
to be tossed away without thought
just as the details of the story itself—
it might have been *The Fall Guy*
or *Four Frightened Women* or *Weekend with Death*—
were quickly forgotten by each of the soldiers
who had clung to those words as to the side of a life raft
but afterwards didn't even need to make an effort
not to forget what was already being erased,

2

in the diminishing light the elements of the story
popped and went out, it could have been the one
about the missing will or the missing person,
the blackmailed movie star, the body
in the locked room, the wronged convict

looking for payback from the man who sent him up,
the voice rasping threats in the dark after midnight,
the rattling of the bolted storm window,
the redhead with a yen for trombone players,
the tennis pro hiding more than one disgraceful secret,
the Scotch and soda that didn't taste quite right,
what the hat check girl from Club Esquire
whispered to the owner's bullnecked chauffeur,
the fallen hairnet, the half-smoked cigarette,
the galoshes still dry after the rainstorm,
the bent key slipped into the green handbag,
the silk nightgown tossed in the hamper
the way no woman ever would,
but the killer didn't know that—

3

and by then the exhausted soldier has dropped
into a place where not even a Scotch and soda
can help him keep the tell-tale trace
from melting in his hands
while the mind struggles to reassemble
a story with the same name but a different plot—
and by now even the name has changed,
maybe it has become *Ghost of the Shower Handle*
or *Green Horses* or *The Tangled Beans*—
but it hits a skid from the get-go, spins out
into a different century with freakish weather,
where a body with anomalous biological traits
inhabits a zone of methane baths,
in swift eely leaps transmuting the story of anybody
to the story of nobody or more strictly no body,
the dream becoming a commemorative album
on the death of the dreamer
just as he crashes into the brittle wall of light

4

coughing and flicking shards away
and wondering whether dreams
are failed attempts at storytelling,
what with their all too familiar technique
of digression within digression
yanking always further from a main thread
not to be found again, lost
beyond naming, or on the other hand
are stories inadequate attempts
to approximate the dream experience,
imposing a wide-awake logic that will always
remain alien to what it most wanted to capture?
The dreams of the dead have left no trace
but how their stories have piled up, stories of legacies
and massacres and rudely interrupted house calls,
it might have been *The Tale of the Mistaken Twins*
or *The Chastised Wife* or *The Fate of the Orphan*,
judges compiling death sentences for a secret court,
rustled cattle, talking fish, luminescent blossoms,
nothing finally but ordinances and omens,
vows and curses, challenges and predictions,
messages carried by wind across water
to the far shore where they are broadcast like thunder,
louder than any sound in any dream—

5

the dream in a story about a dream
being more elegant than any ever actually dreamt,
the twin dreams for example in the *Arabian Nights* tale
of the impoverished Bagdad merchant
to whom in sleep a messenger appeared
saying 'go to Cairo to find a great treasure'
and who arriving without resources
fell asleep in a mosque where a robbery took place

and being mistaken for a robber was beaten and abused
until the police chief asked him why he came to Cairo
and he related his dream and the police chief uproariously amused
by the gullibility of anyone who would put faith in a dream
told him how he once had more or less the same dream
instructing him urgently to go to Bagdad
to a house described in meticulous detail which the merchant
silently recognised as being none other than his own
and on returning to his homeland obeyed the instruction
to excavate the fountain at the end of the garden
thereby uncovering the predicted treasure,
no story could be neater, its crisscross pattern
even cancels itself out leaving no mess behind
as if it were literally the story to end all stories,
as if finally there had been enough stories—
except that this evidently cannot be the case
since when that moment threatens to arrive
it only generates a further story,
a story about precisely the end of all stories
and that turns out to be merely the overture
to the multivolume saga *The End of All Things*
that will generate spinoffs and prequels
and heavily promoted follow-ups
of which *Part Twelve: Beyond Nothing*
will serve as teaser for *My End Is My Beginning*—

6

This had been going on longer
than anyone was in a position to remember,
there was not even a name for the tribe of humans
who over a period of seventeen thousand years
had inhabited continuously a cave
fifty feet wide and five hundred feet long
yet you might be permitted to imagine
that in all that time nobody dropped the ball
as they practised in the dark rearranging plot points

deleting kinks and dead spots along the way
like a story conference lasting millennia

7

and when having emerged to the light
they invented theatre
the principals went into their dance
dressed up as lovers who hyperbolise and are forgiven
as lovers who are not forgiven and are slaughtered
as lecherous servants who always
in some sideways fashion speak truth
skinflints who rage and are mocked
bandits who triumph through disguise
brothel keepers who smuggle messages
clowns who stagger through alleyways
knocking over buckets and fruit stands
householders who tremble for fear of thieves
girls too beautiful to be hidden
warriors turned monstrous from lust
crones who explicate lost bloodlines
a procession of stick figures
and their living shadows
each both itself and
the opposite of the other
unsolvable mixtures
ghosts who sing
animals who prophesy
chasms that open in the ground
to show where the wealth was hidden
long before the story began
just so there would be something or other to restore—

8

millennia of disconnected anecdotes
like my uncle told about a drunken brawl
at Coney Island or a three-day blizzard

or a school chum dying of sepsis
from a dirty jackknife, figments of a gone world
for which the story is no substitute—
the story is nothing
or not more than the length of thick celluloid
by which a professional burglar pries his way
into the closet where the stash is, not more
than the weather they moved around in
all the while they were telling it,
not more than what hangs on it,
props, perfumes, backtalk, smoke,
the crinkling sound from the adjacent room
reachable by no other method
and not even then—

9

as the child found who, trying to decide
which Classic Comic to read when he had read them all,
hoping to find one that would still—
still and always—seem new even after
it was more familiar than his hand turning the pages—
it might have been *Lorna Doone* or *The Talisman*
or *Tom Brown's School Days*—told himself
'I want a story that is not like a trap'—
as he started to fear that every story
is a trap that lures past the greenery of the entryway
into aisles ever narrowing,
whether of barracks or churchyard or schoolroom,
without hope of a reverse manoeuvre—
and so went poking along the seams of the stories
for the empty space,
the green and dripping glistening light
of the place where the story stands still—
Deerslayer's Glimmerglass or the endless Siberia
of Michael Strogoff—the zone of unending interlude
where the travellers have lunch and savour guitar music

and because the story has stopped
they never in the end resume their journey
and consequently are spared
the drought-ridden badlands
plagues slag heaps corrupt marauders
tax collectors torturers slavedrivers
blighted orphanages airless chapels
the confusions and betrayals
waiting for all who manage to reach the city—

10

I don't remember where I heard that story
and certainly it has changed beyond recognition
I remember hearing about a person
who sat down once a year
to write down the details of the particularly
disturbing incident that had haunted a lifetime
choosing to write them down without ever consulting
the earlier drafts and at the end of many decades
laid them side by side to find
a suite of unrecognisably different stories,
nothing remaining but arbitrary narratives
so blatantly concocted as to be beyond belief
yet no less true since there they are,
they never go away—
by their very survival
they confirm there are no untrue stories,
there is nothing *but* truth,
it occupies every point of space,
seals the exits, the wallpaper is made of it,
the accumulation of foxed and partly shredded
childhood storybooks is made of it, the orange sun
going down out on the street is made of it,
even for the bystander perched outside it
the outsideness is made of it, what doesn't
fit into it is tangled in its main works,

11

while meanwhile—back at the ranch
as my uncle would have said—
even as the story was being ironed out
the thing that actually happened went off
on its own tangent, it did happen,
it did, there *was* a sun in the street
but once only, such being the monstrous condition
imposed on the living who find relief only
in the story that can be taken as needed
even though each telling alters it,
yet after all the freedom to alter it
is what makes it a story, it wouldn't
amount to much without the malleability
that comes close to the heart of ecstatic delight,
while the event—the jackknife
or the brutal happening at Coney Island—
stays locked up in its truth, warehouse beyond access,
it would not be truth if it were not inaccessible,
if they could touch it they would change it,
they do change it and it is no more,
and spend the remainder of their time
wondering where it went, that incident
which was purity itself and since purity
is beyond them it bedevils them
until they make or stumble upon
a story to be a stand-in
like a puppet or a candle
a splash of indigo
a stain a mere splinter
a signal going off in the air
a signal going off the air—

12

you want to hear it
you're afraid to hear it

you're tired of hearing it
you tell it to yourself
you imagine others telling it to themselves
you want to hear it again over and over
you've never heard it
it has been deliberately kept from you
you would pay to hear it
you wish you hadn't heard it
you would pay to forget it
you heard it but you can't remember it
no one ever heard it
it has never been told
it tells itself
it will be telling itself with no one left to hear

Fabricating Texts for Theatre from a Tribal Village in Bengal

Jean-Frédéric Chevallier

'She is completely different. What she likes the most are word combinations.'
                                                Federico Fellini, *La Dolce Vita* (1960)

'Oh yes, okay: it's about talking to each other as if words were sounds and matter.'
                                             Jean-Luc Godard, *La Chinoise* (1967)

Imagine a street, or better still—this one being less than four metres wide—imagine a narrow road made of hard-packed reddish soil stretched over about a kilometre, and lined on both sides with one- or two-storey mud houses shaded by majestic trees. Often, chickens, buffaloes, calves, a few goats and some blackish-muddy pigs roam along it. Early morning, as well as late afternoon, scantily clad children, especially boys, play marbles on it, bows and arrows, or—with old inner tubes recovered from their parents' cycles—roll hoops. All day long, girls in brightly coloured tunics and women in garish saris wind up it, carrying newborns on their hips or the water they have just drawn from the well. Late at night, between October and March, elephants cross it in search of paddy delicacies and fermented drinks.

    This street is Borotalpada,[39] a remote village in Bengal whose denizens speak Santhali.[40]

---

[39] Cf., https://trimukhiplatform.org/borotalpada.
[40] Santhali belongs to the Munda subfamily of Austro-Asiatic languages. It is spoken

The Santhals are the largest aboriginal group in India. In the state of West Bengal, there are about two-and-a-half million. In Borotalpada there are exactly half a thousand.

Almost every Borotalpadian is a 'BPL' (below poverty line) card holder entitled to some subsidies both in kind and cash in return for accepting the implementation of policies which are half the time inaccurate. However, the young go to school, the teenagers to boarding school, while to continue studying girls receive from the local government small monthly stipends insofar as their parents don't use the money for covering the remaining expenses of their brothers' marriage. Each family owns plots of land to grow paddy, producing enough rice at least to feed themselves throughout the year. Many sell about 20 per cent of their harvest at the local weekly market. Hospital admissions are free (the recently built establishment being six kilometres away) but not the medicines.

With a dozen families from Borotalpada, art producer Sukla Bar and I have been, since 2008, preparing and showcasing performances and installations. They take place in the open, inside the village itself or on its outskirts. They combine contemporary dance-theatre, video and sound arts, wall, facade, esplanade, path, jungle, grove, lake or stone quarry.

In these artworks we composed together, often text is involved. Text that we can put under the category of 'literature': first because it is composed with words and second because it is composed with an artistic purpose in sight. A simple definition of 'literature' being: a combination of words, often written, used with an artistic purpose.[41]

Speaking about 'literature' is a way to say that we haven't been preparing pedagogical texts to read in a conference, treatises to print

---

by around eight million people in India (in the states of Assam, Bihar, Jharkhand, Mizoram, Odisha, Tripura and West Bengal), Bangladesh, Bhutan and Nepal.

[41] Having in mind, of course, that 'neither Virgil, nor Shakespeare, nor Cao Xueqin, the Chinese author of *The Dream in the Red Flag*, have the word literature or at least an exact equivalent, and [that] bringing together texts as distant as the Assyro-Babylonian "literature", troubadours' poems, Wattpad fan-fictions and Baudelaire's literary programme is not an obvious gesture, the distorting effects of which cannot be underestimated'. Alexandre Gefen, *L'Idée de la littérature. de l'art pour l'art aux écritures d'interventions* (Paris: Corti, 2021), p. 77.

in a book, sociological studies for academic purposes or welfare policy implementation.

Claude Simon insisted, in his acceptance lecture for his Nobel Prize in Literature, that when writing a novel, he has nothing to say. And he added:

> As a literary author, I have nothing to say. Even if some important truth of a social, historical, or sacred nature had been revealed to me, it would have seemed to me a burlesque proceeding, at the very least, to have used [literature] to express it, rather than a reasoned philosophical, sociological, or theological thesis.[42]

Some years later, he shared an amusing and clarifying anecdote:

> Invited to Moscow by the Union of Writers of the USSR (it was before Gorbachev), I underwent a strange type of interrogation at their headquarters, during which, among other questions, I was asked what were the main problems that I faced [as a writer]. I then replied that I could count three such problems. The first, starting a sentence; the second, continuing it; the third, ending it. [A reply] which, as one might guess, cast a chill around me.[43]

For example, when writing the novel *The Acacia*, Claude Simon had to spend a long time looking for a proper way to complete a sentence which dealt with a pyramidal pile of objects and bodies. He finally managed to find a term that combined efficiently with earlier words. To his surprise, this term was 'bicycle' and had very little to do with the beginning and middle of the phrase. On the contrary, it was introducing a distance.

In Borotalpada, we are operating in the same way: rehearsing different texts, composing new parts when some previous ones are not efficient enough for our taste, modifying sentences, words, punctuation, even languages: this paragraph in Santhali instead of

---

[42] Nobel Lecture on 9 December 1985. Claude Simon, *Discours de Stockholm* (Paris: Minuit, 1986), p. 24.
[43] Claude Simon, '*Littérature et mémoire*' in *Quatre Conférences* (Paris: Minuit, 2012), p. 123.

English, that phrase in French instead of Bengali. We increase or decrease verbal distances and observe what then is produced or not produced. We arrange, rearrange, change the layouts of words until getting finally an artefact that we hope may work.

With the years passing, it appears that of such a strange 'literature', of this tinkered with, unstable, non-definitive and moving 'literary' practice that is ours, we can propose a typology. A typology that would distinguish between both, the effect each kind of text may produce on the spectators-listeners or readers, and their respective roles within our art pieces.

Of course, as it's all about today's arts, the senses are involved.[44] But it's more: once fully unfolded, my typology will highlight a gradation towards nonsense—a cheerful, stimulating, uplifting nonsense which consists in arousing, through words, a diversity of *unmainstreamed* desires.

ANNOUNCING

[*With a microphone; the performer, sitting on a bicycle, is wearing sunglasses.*] We are faced with a problem: usually, when we put on a theatre performance, we have nothing to express, no message to convey nor history to tell. But this time the situation is different: twelve months ago, Chumki went to Paradise. Five months ago, Kajol joined her. For this reason, here and now we would like to try building things a little differently.[45]

[*With a megaphone; wearing a diving mask, the performer is standing in the middle of a large open field.*] Please do come and sit near the water. We need the dusk light to begin. Thank you.[46]

Here you have two texts that you understand from beginning to end, texts that seem to have been composed only for that purpose: to

---

[44] I have developed this point in 'From Senses to Sense: The Arts of Presenting', *Fabrique de l'art*, no. 2, Calcutta, Trimukhi Platform, 2016, pp. 26–41.

[45] *Essay on Seasonal Variation in Santhal Society* (2016–2017). It's a text that I said. Cf. https://trimukhiplatform.org/essayonseasonalvariationinsanthalsociety and https://youtu.be/9idq234fd0w (0:38).

[46] *Jol i Jibon* (2018). Text said by Ramjit Hansda. Cf. https://trimukhiplatform.org/jolijibon.

be understood. They could be called *announcement-texts*: texts that, by announcing something, create expectations in the mind of the audience. Expectations that, of course, can be thwarted, deceived or twisted; otherwise there would be no point in resorting to these poorly made texts. By generating expectation, the words create an attention towards what is coming next, though it has nothing to do with what the *announcement-text* seemed to have been announcing.

In the sequence that follows the saying of the first text, four Santhals, aged nine to eighteen, eat Chinese noodles—which they usually do not do—first using chopsticks as in East Asian countries and then forks as in Europe or North America—which they normally never do: in Borotalpada, you eat with your right hand![47] And during the sequence that follows the saying of the second text, night has already fallen.

Both texts are signals that do not signal anything, or at least very little. They give indications that indicate almost nothing. By doing so, they help the spectators not only not to worry about what is happening next but also to look at it with an active attention.

With the help of Sukla Bar, I drafted these texts in Bengali a few days before starting the rehearsals in the village. On other occasions, we take from texts that I wrote ten or twenty years ago, in Paris, for example, or in Calcutta more recently, that is to say writings which weren't originally meant to enrich one or the other of our dance-theatre performances.

Whatever the way, during rehearsals in Borotalpada, because these texts are likely to be of some use for us, we translate them into Bengali and Santhali. Then they are 'said' by several performers from the team. They are put in different mouths, tried in a diversity of textures, tones and flow of voices. If a text thus put to the test seems finally to 'fit' in the artwork, then all that remains is to re-specify certain expressions, remove others or change the sentence order. What mainly guides us are questions of sound and rhythm.

---

[47] Cf. Jean-Frédéric Chevallier, 'Theatre Relations: From a Tribal Village in India', *Fabrique de l'art*, no. 3/4, Calcutta, Trimukhi Platform, 2018, pp. 148–153.

QUESTIONING

[*The actress with her back to the lake is facing the audience.*] In the dark, do not think without ceasing thinking for your children, that your children, only your children, are your children. Otherwise everything would go from bad to worse and it would be too bad for you. Do not die tonight. You could lose your teeth and that would be too bad for you. Do not leave without telling me why you stay.[48]

[*With a microphone; the actress's bust and face appear through a window a few metres above the spectators whom she is looking in the eye.*] I would like you to make a hole in you, with water and salt, for me, and from the ground with your key, to open the door of your room.[49]

Here again are texts that everyone can understand: they are said in Bengali, a language known by the Adivasi villagers as well as by the audience from Calcutta. But, though everyone can understand them, these texts do not convey a clear meaning. On the contrary, it's their strangeness and inchoateness that first strike the listeners. These are bizarre arrangements of words which—as one does not fully comprehend them—put him or her in an unstable position where somehow he or she is forced to think.

I call them *question-texts*: series of words that invite each member of the audience to question herself or himself. The questions one asks oneself may concern the text that one is listening to or reading. It may well concern what one is experimenting with at that moment. And it may concern something that has nothing to do with the text or with the performance. Because the interrogations at stake here are personal ones.

About two months after having seen *Guignol's Dol* (from which the first series is extracted), Indrani Mallick gave me interesting details about her experience:

---

[48] *Guignol's Dol* (2012). Text written by me and said by Surojmoni Hansda. Cf. https://trimukhiplatform.org/guignolsdol and https://youtu.be/EPeknG5MleE (1:26).

[49] *Homemade Theatre* (2019). Text written by me and said by Sumita Besra. Cf. https://trimukhiplatform.org/homemadetheatre. Version, slightly different, at Goethe-Institut Calcutta: https://youtu.be/qAuZoDF9jnM (39:32).

It is very difficult to foresee what the future holds. Certainly, there is a halo of light, at a distance, that one hardly perceives, but this light is shrouded by darkness: there is no distinction in the features. What will happen to us can be good or can be bad, we can't know. Such an uncertainty produces a disturbance which becomes a distress. When I hear 'you could lose your teeth', I understand that one is always in danger of losing the aesthetic of life: to be without teeth is to be without beauty, it's to continue living but with a spirit already dead.[50]

Here the spectator is doing something other than identifying a pre-established signification. The text doesn't communicate a meaning but produces inner sensations. What seems to be relevant for Indrani is what she experiences and feels while listening: what she says to herself while experiencing and feeling what she is experiencing and feeling while hearing this series of words.

Nevertheless, when Indrani hears, '*Do not think without ceasing thinking for your children, that your children, only your children, are your children*', the course of her thinking bends. The open uncertainty she was experiencing now concerns exclusively the education of her children—two young adults studying graphic arts—'*was it a good thing,*' she asks herself, '*to have pushed them to spend their days painting and drawing?*' The trouble is no more multiple but focused on that one question; it is reduced to it.

Is the sentence over-orienting feelings and thoughts? For it took a few words to steer Indrani's reflection in a given direction, disregarding other possible courses.

Sometimes the performance title itself imposes. In eleven of the fourteen testimonies collected from the audience after the premiere of *My Body Is Another Landscape*, the 'landscape' was mentioned. Was this a proof of the great accuracy of the name or a sign of a drastic limitation in the number of ways that there would have been to experience the artwork?

---

[50] Testimony shared with me during a phone conversation in March 2012 in Calcutta.

QUESTIONING LITERALLY OR DISTRACTING

To avoid this pitfall, sometimes we literally compose a series of questions: a succession of interrogations that invites thought to be set in motion, but playing with variations so as not to assign to it any identifiable goal.

> [*With a microphone; the actress sits on a bed of rope, close to vapoured smoke wisps escaping from a fire of dried leaves; her face is turned towards the audience; an actor rests his head on her lap.*] Did you ever see that huge black pig riding a shiny motorcycle while flipping through an outdated textbook? When you were two years old, were you already thinking about getting married? Did you catch a glimpse of an ocean liner sinking in the lake of Borotalpada the very day Kajol was chatting in French with Jean-Frédéric? Would you prefer to eat beef or to eat yourself? Can a dog climb a rice stalk? Do you really want to live?[51]

On this occasion, the text is composed in the course of the rehearsal. The first part of the performance is more or less defined and we are wondering how to continue. After a few trials, we discover that asking strange questions could work. So we need to choose what questions to keep, what questions to modify, what questions to add, and in which order.

I elaborated on part of these questions, let's say the 'speculative' part, and Dhani Hansda (she was at that time seventeen) covered the more 'down to earth' one. We translated and retranslated everything together, from Bengali to Santhali and from Santhali to Bengali. Passing from one language to another helped us to sharpen the formulations and to ensure both their diversity and the intriguing dimension of the whole. Once or twice we mixed Dhani's series with mine. In this line for example: '*Would you prefer to eat beef or to eat yourself?*'[52] Ultimately, the explosion of points of view, the disturbing

---

[51] *Essay on Seasonal Variation in Santhal Society* (2016–2017). Text said by Dhani Hansda. Cf. https://youtu.be/NeoBcl8vQI8 (3:41).

[52] It's a question which, we didn't know at that time, echoes a famous one formulated by philosopher Donna J. Haraway: 'Critters interpenetrate one another, loop around

strangeness of the assemblage would provide, I hoped, a plurality of listenings.

DENSIFYING SO AS TO SEND THINKING ELSEWHERE

In seeking to guarantee a diversity of experiences, sometimes we didn't operate through dispersion but through extreme densification. A dance-theatre intervention carried out in the gardens of the French Institute in New Delhi has for a title the following sentences:

> You feel the flow stopping, then starting again, going straight, bending, turning and drawing circles, and finally being appeased. These are neither images nor sounds, but a rhythm that, in moments, simulates both at the same time. Then, only then you begin to perceive a city, a village, a home. [*Projected on the left side on the facade of the French Institute, on the right side on a large screen, the dancers moving under the arches in between.*][53]

I would call such a combination of phrases a *words wall*: a composition of sentences so strongly full (neither uniform nor daunting but with no cracks and no hole to slip into) that hearing it, the spectator almost immediately will feel not weary but compelled to leave and go thinking elsewhere (figuratively speaking). The text is taken from Peter Handke's *Short Letter for a Long Farewell*[54] and slightly modified: I replaced 'I' with 'you' and added 'village' and 'home'. A month later, when this first stage draft became a complete dance-theatre performance to be premiered in Borotalpada, another extract, this one taken from 'Of the Refrain' by Gilles Deleuze and Félix Guattari, was transformed at a much greater range.

---

and through one another, eat each other, get indigestion, and partially digest and partially assimilate one another, and thereby establish *sympoietic* arrangements.' *Staying with the Trouble: Making Kin in the Chthulucene* (London: Duke University Press, 2016), p. 58.

[53] It was on 31 January 2019, on the occasion of the *Night of Ideas*, Cf. https://trimukhiplatform.org/youfeeltheflow and https://youtu.be/nICiYya6h3Y (1:32).

[54] Cf. Peter Handke, *La Courte lettre pour un long adieu*, (Paris: Gallimard, 'Folio', 1997), p. 45. My translation.

[*Speaking into a microphone, the actress twirls a low-intensity light bulb.*] You are a child. You are in the dark. You are gripped with fear. You comfort yourself by singing. You sing under your breath. You walk and halt to your song. Lost, you take shelter and orient yourself with your little song.

You are at home now but your home does not preexist. You had to draw a circle around that uncertain and fragile centre, to organise a limited space.

Many, very diverse, components have a part in this. You are a sound artist: you combine sonic bricks. You are a child: you hum to summon the strength for the schoolwork you have to hand in. You are a housewife: you sing to yourself, or listen to the radio, as you marshal the anti-chaos forces of your work.

Before destroying your home, you have to build your house. Go on moving, with your eyes blinking. Listen to the song you sing. Because you sing a song that is not a song. Bricks after bricks, layers after layers, it is your home.[55]

In view of the original, the above series has been shortened, diverted and extended. The process was gradual. For the draft in New Delhi, while 'you' substituted for 'he' or 'she', cuts and additions remained limited. It was in passing from English to Bengali, and from one mouth to another, that the textual composition started to be really transformed. A tribal actress from Borotalpada (who expressed the desire to proclaim Deleuze and Guattari's phrases) took over the 'role' played in New Delhi by a Calcuttan dancer. The rewriting took into account the villager's speech flow and the importance she attached to being understood by her fellow villagers (who, Bengali not being their mother tongue, have a limited vocabulary). It took also into account my concern for the rhythm of the Bengali grammatical structures as well as the sounding of certain substantives and adjectives in this language. It was not a question of simplifying the series of words but of passing it through a process which in chemistry

---

[55] Partly modified extracts taken from Gilles Deleuze, Félix Guattari, *A Thousand Plateaus: Capitalism and Schizophrenia* (London: University of Minnesota Press, 1987), pp. 311–312. My translation.

would be called *reduction*.⁵⁶ It was important to ensure a maximum philosophical density and to reach a kind of stimulative hermeticism that would be welcoming because it is exciting. In this sense, the *words wall* is the exact opposite of a focus point. With the *wall*, each member of the audience is focusing on a series of words that cannot be focused on. By doing so, one is carried along towards defocusing and then refocusing, at will and taste, in other directions. Instead of thinking about 'refrain', one thinks of what one wants. Obviously, the literary plasticity of the original text (let's say, the Deleuze-Guattari style) greatly facilitates these unforeseen changes in usage.

And it seemed to have worked quite well as, among the many spectators who shared their impressions, only one (Aheli Halder) made reference to the notions of 'house' and 'home'.⁵⁷

Important point: while Dhani Hansda was enumerating questions in Santhali or Sumita Besra uttering in Bengali a *reduced* passage inspired by *A Thousand Plateaus*, translations were projected, respectively, on the ground in front and on the wall behind the performer. Thus, each one in the audience, whatever the languages she or he was comfortable with, had the opportunity to weave her or his own lines of flight.

TROUBLING / DIFFERENTIATING / LINKING

There are cases where not everyone can grasp the meaning of the words. Only a part of the audience is able to do it.

OKOYAG CHÈD ÉIDARI. AKODOKO MONÉ KA AA ALEYAG NOWA DO. APEYAG DO JIBON RE BANG. BANG HUYUG AA AR BANG HUYUG AA. CHED ÉIDARI TAPÉ NODÉ AR NODÉ. INJ DO ADIVASHI SANTHAL KURI KINJI. MENKHAN EKDOM APE JHOTO CHITI BITI PEYA. INJ THE DO NOKAN AASPORDA BANG BARAG TAPEYA. EKAL BANGA. EKAL BANGA. EKAL BANGA.⁵⁸

---

⁵⁶ In chemistry, a reduction is any of a class of chemical reactions in which the number of electrons associated with an atom or a group of atoms is increased.
⁵⁷ Cf. http://youtu.be/bNs4pxP82HA (2:54).
⁵⁸ *The Thing That Exists When We Aren't There* (2013): https://trimukhiplatform.org/thethingthatexistswhenwearentthere.

The purpose of the transcription in capital letters in Latin alphabet is to give you an idea of the sounds of the Santhali. Some indications of pronunciation: E corresponds to the sound 'é' in French and 'e' in Bengali, U and R respectively to the sound 'u' and to a rolled 'r' in Bengali and Spanish. I further suggest interrupting your reading for a moment and watching twenty seconds of the following video clip: https://youtu.be/Zqvvq-DPsB0, starting at the second minute, eleventh second.[59]

This is another case of a text made during rehearsals on the same principle as for Dhani's: something seems to work so we develop it, unfolding it until we get a text whose structure, duration, rhythm are suitable for this or that moment of the performance. It is Kajol Hansda who composed this words series and it is she who says it. As she did not write it (not knowing how to write), she memorised it while she was elaborating it. As her composition is in Santhali, and we purposely don't project any subtitles, only one part of the audience understands it. In February 2013 in Borotalpada, around hundred and fifty people got what Kajol was saying: the audience from the village and from the surrounding Santhal area. And a hundred people approximately did not understand anything: the audience from Calcutta, the guest artists from abroad involved in the festival and the Bengali inhabitants of the local area (there are also Bengali villages in the tribal area from where we operate).

What is the point of sharing words if they cannot be understood by everyone?[60] It is that, behind the apparent aberration of the gesture, there is a bet. If what is called 'audience' or 'public' does not consist of a whole in the sense of a closed, uniform and coherent entity but a heterogeneous assembly, an agency of dissimilar people, then the function of such a text would be to activate, to accentuate,

---

[59] Direct access: https://youtu.be/Zqvvq-DPsB0&t=131.

[60] Students from Comparative Literature at Jadavpur University once complained to me: 'When you are trying to use language you are actually trying to produce some meaning. Those are not nonsense words. They have some meaning, in French or in Santhali. But we cannot understand the language so the meaning is not coming through to us.' (Ariane Mnouchkine, Jean-Frédéric Chevallier, Samantak Das, Budhray Besra, 'Theatre Today', *Fabrique de l'art*, no. 3/4, *op. cit.*, p. 167.)

to enhance some of their differences. A *differences-accentuator-text*. Differences that disappear when the text finishes. When, after her proclamation, Kajol moans, rubs her face, and sits down, all the spectators witness the same series of actions: there is no difference at all among the audience. But before, while she was speaking, there were huge differences between those who could employ the language she was using and those who, somehow unoccupied, were helpless in doing so. This difference in positions led to different ways of being present.

Obviously, to get such a text to work properly, it's preferable to have a diversity of people among the audience, people from different geographical origins, habits, social backgrounds, etc. Maybe such a text only awakens differences already present among the audience. Anyway, it is thanks to this combination of differences that the text produces a second kind of effect: an invitation to build links between different presences. Because Kajol's text is of a special kind: it's an affective manifesto. She is telling (almost shouting at) her fellow tribal villagers:

> Who has the right and what right? You said to yourself 'this is ours!' but it's not up to you. Nothing, ever, is yours. Nothing. What is yours here today? I, a daughter of Santhals, will tear you to pieces. I won't let grow your claim to own and to exclude, never. These people from abroad and from Calcutta who are now present among us, they will be always welcome in my house. Welcoming them in our homes is being true to ourselves.[61]

As you can imagine, that night, such a declaration had a strong effect on the Santhal audience. Partly because of the way Kajol was performing, partly because she was an elderly person to whom, following Santhal traditions, one has to listen and whose views one has to respect.

So here is a text that not only works on creating different ways of being present but also works on putting into relationships these different presences. A *relation-text*. A text requesting part of

---

[61] Translation by Dhananjoy Hansda and Chandrai Murmu.

the audience to enter into relationships with another part of the audience, a different part. A text that invites us to focus attention on the issue of co-presence. Because, obviously, even for those who didn't understand Santhali, something in the audience around was changing: they could easily perceive it.

As director of the piece, I didn't ask for the meaning of the text. It never came to my mind to do so. As we rehearsed, besides Kajol trusting my choices and me trusting hers, I could tell that the text had found its form and rhythm. I knew well enough that something deep was happening. I did not need more to do my work. And if finally I got it translated, it was after the premiere, and because the impact on the villagers had been so strong that one of them felt that he should share it with me.

The fact is, the tirade would not have produced its effects if everyone in the audience had understood it. It would have become a life lesson or lecture imposed on an artificially homogeneous public. If the perception of words becomes the same for all, the text loses its literary characteristics and fails to produce its aesthetic effects.

It's true also that these words were specially troubling. It was this trouble that was activating the *differentiator* behaviour.[62] It was because some spectators were first troubled that they worked on differentiating, and then on weaving relationships.

Let's take another sample, maybe a more explicit one. During a lightning stage work in Calcutta designed with a group of students from Jadavpur University, I suggested to Abhirupa Haldar, Ananya Kanjilal and Indrasena Mukhopadhyay to whisper in Bengali in the ears of some of the spectators the following sentences:

> If you would be me and I would be you, what would you do if I would tell you that I want to sleep with you otherwise I would die … because my desire for you is so great that it cannot deceive you,

---

[62] Here also it would be interesting to enrich my analysis with the conceptual propositions made by Donna J. Haraway in *Staying with the Trouble* (*op. cit.*): 'Each time I trace a tangle and add a few threads that at first seemed whimsical but turned out to be essential to the fabric, I get a bit straighter that staying with the trouble of complex worlding is the name of the game of living and dying well together' (p. 29).

neither can you go wrong on my intention which is to see you at the peak of joy in my arms?[63]

Regarding the dynamics at stake in the usage of words, there are, as in Kajol's text: (1) a partiality, (2) an 'us', (3) a trouble, (4) a differentiation or activation of the differences (a disassembling by underlining dissimilarities), (5) an increase of the trouble due to this activation and, from there, (6) a duplication of the differentiating process, leading to (7) a deep concern for weaving relationships.

A partiality because the words are addressed only to certain spectators: those living in a Santhal village or those to whom an actress chooses to whisper. An 'us' because the words establish a 'you people and me' or a 'you seductive one and me'. The 'us' includes the person who speaks and each of those who hear her, in the double sense of perceiving sounds and understanding words. A trouble, on the one hand, because the constitution of this 'us' establishes both an exclusive intimacy (with regard to other spectators who do not know the language or to whom nobody has whispered in the ear) and an intimacy without proximity (particularly in the second case). A trouble, on the other hand, because the wording is destabilising (*'nothing, ever, is yours [...] and I will tear you to pieces'*) or abruptly opened (*'what would you do if I would tell you that I want to sleep with you'*).[64] A differentiation follows which leads those who are now troubled to see others differently: *'What would this man from Calcutta sitting next to me on the plastic tarp*

---

[63] *R/T Poetry 1 (Bulky Body Deduction)* (2011). Cf. https://fr.trimukhiplatform.org/rtpoetry1 and https://youtu.be/9VJbVllciFU (8:40). I wrote these lines in the middle of the 1990s for two different performances I was directing at La Grande Bouvêche in Orsay, France. The same text was then used, in French and Spanish, for another performance I directed and which was showcased in Mexico City from 2005 to 2007: see *infra* 'Diversifying Experiences'.

[64] The trouble is in reality of more than two sorts. After watching three of our performances (one in Borotalpada and two in Calcutta), a student from Jadavpur University shared with us the following: 'There seems to be a conscious playfulness with meaning, with the semantic meaning of the performance text that you create. Is that not a problem? You are moving away from the symmetry of meaning, you want everybody to interpret things in their own way, so sometimes the ambiguity is disturbing me because it doesn't match with logical reasoning.' (A. Mnouchkine, J-F. Chevallier, S. Das, B. Besra, 'Theatre Today', *op. cit.*, pp. 163–164.)

think if he knew what has just been yelled at us villagers?', 'What would my lover say on learning what this pretty girl was whispering to me?' A dissimilarity is posited, almost imposed, but in a strict and broad sense. There is neither opposition nor conflict between the dissimilar. Simply, as one would easily be able to distinguish between the living beings who perceive infrared or ultraviolet and those who do not, the former suddenly realise that the latter have seen neither of these two colours. The process of differentiation is redoubled when those who have not been troubled by the words nevertheless perceive in those who have been the symptoms of their trouble and in return see them differently: *'What is happening to them?'* the last ones will ask. The process ultimately offers the possibility of weaving relationships: *'These other dissimilar people who, by differentiating them from us, have been given back their distance from ourselves, well, we also want to be in a relationship with them'.*

DELAYING THE MOMENT OF UNDERSTANDING

The strategy can gain in complexity so as to build a text that everyone ends up understanding, but later. Not because the formulations are abstruse and it is necessary to take time to assimilate them to later deduce their original meaning, but because the wording would be organised in such a manner that comprehension cannot but be delayed, for some people or for all. In *Jol i Jibon / Life in the Water*, spectators will first hear in Santhali:

> [*With a microphone; the actress is half kneeling on a large wooden table arranged in a lake.*] GNÈLMÉ. ALOM GNÉLA. TANGUÏMÉ. OKTO ALOM BILOMA. TANGI ALOM TAHÉNA. KUHU KUHU MÉ. CHÉRO BÉROMÉ. POT POTAMÉ. LANDAÏMÉ. DJALKAOMÉ. KULIYMÉ. [*With a microphone; the actor is lying under the table, his body partially in the water.*] ALOM KULÏA. ALOM KULI KOA. LANDAÏMÉ. NITOHO LANDAÏMÉ. INEGÉ. NASÉ TCHAHABMÉ. INE KHAN BITIRKO GNÈLA. INE TAÏOM SAHAMÉ.[65]

---

[65] *Jol i Jibon* (2018): https://trimukhiplatform.org/jolijibon and https://youtu.be/RpV0VKWhYmI (6:51).

Here again, those among the audience who were Santhalophones listened to the words, and those who were not, heard sounds. But, ten minutes later, two actors say in Bengali:

> [*Through microphones; the actress sits under the table, her legs in the water; the actor is seated on a stool at the right side of the table.*] Look. Don't look. Wait. Don't waste your time. Don't wait. Coo. Babble, chatter, smile, give light. Ask. Don't ask, don't ask anything. Smile. This time, yes, smile. Stop smiling. Open slightly your mouth, the lips of your fingers. Let them see inside. And then get out.[66]

Now, in addition to the Santhalophones, there are also the Bengalophones who understand what has been said. And, the former speaking roughly the language of the latter, they easily see that it is the same text, but translated. So far, only those who do not know Santhali or Bengali remain without having understood anything. About ten minutes elapse and subtitles appear in French and English. At that point, everyone in the audience has understood.

Here, the series structure imposes a delay in the comprehension. Short or long, the delay is sometimes necessary as it is a condition, so something significant may happen to the audience. In his essay, *Post-dramatic Theatre*, Hans-Thies Lehmann insisted on the process:

> It's important here that we don't understand everything at once. We go by the principle that the meaning remains deferred. The accessory and the apparently non-significant are exactly recorded precisely because, in their apparent meaninglessness, they can become heavily meaningful.[67]

It is not, as was the case with the *words wall*, that the audience is looking away; it's just that one looks and listens differently. It is the

---

[66] Text said by Chintamoni Hansda, Ramjit Hansda and Surojmoni Hansda. Cf. https://youtu.be/RpV0VKWhYmI (10:53). I composed the text with extracts from poems I had written long before. Sukla Bar and I translated them into Bengali, then with the team in Santhali. To read the full text, cf. 'জল ই জীবন | *La vie dans l'eau*', *Fabrique de l'art*, no. 3/4, *op. cit.*, pp. 180–189.

[67] Hans-Thies Lehmann, *Le Théâtre postdramatique* (Paris: L'Arche, 2002), p. 137.

quality of the spectators' attention, their availability as much as their sensitivity to the present moment that are sharpened: not only do we see differently the one who says words when we do not understand him or her straight away but we also see differently what surrounds him or her. As philosopher Vinciane Despret pointed out:

> The visual [what we are able to see] participates in the order of certainty (as in the saying: '*you have to see it to believe it*') whereas with a sound, an enigma is created: sound pushes you to go and see, to go see further, it puts you in search. [...] The quest for sound is a quest for curiosity that respects the fact that we do not know everything and that we do not have access to everything. With sounds, we must remain apprentices. [By welcoming sounds this way], we also allow the visual to regain fragility, to lose certainties: everything regarding our relationships both fails and is replayed.[68]

To make this clearer, let's take an arrangement of sentences composed during rehearsals at my request by Pini Soren, then nine years old. Budhray Besra, twenty-four years old, helps her structure the text. From what she says about her day's routine, he chooses the most salient passages and puts them in order in writing. He then translates them into Bengali for me. The preparation of the English subtitles leads me to modify the text, its structure, the lengths of its parts. Budhray carries over these changes to the Santhali version for Pini. Here are the subtitles, projected twelve minutes after the sequence began:

> Her name is Pini. She lives in Borotalpada. She is nine years old. She is the one speaking in front of you.
>   Early morning after waking up she brushes her teeth with a neem twig. She plays a while with her friends then goes to the pond and bathes. When she comes back home to eat, the plates are not washed. She asks why. Her sister-in-law gets angry and sends her to do the dishes. Pini is a little scared. She is sad too but remains silent.

---

[68] Vinciane Despret, 'La grande table des idées', France Culture radio, 23 February 2021.

She eats alone, talks to no one, takes her books and notebooks and starts for school.

On the way she calls her friends so they can go together. They see a snake. Not a big one. Pini says not to kill it. Her friends say to kill it. In the time they spend discussing the matter, the snake takes the opportunity to escape.

They reach school and sit in the classroom. Pini didn't do her homework. The teacher scolds her. She doesn't answer but thinks that whatever the guy says doesn't matter. The teacher asks her to have this homework ready for the next day.

The teacher calls for the midday meal. Everybody sits down to eat rice and curry. Beside Pini there is a little boy. He is crying. The teacher asks Pini what's going on. Pini explains that the reason he's crying is because he doesn't have enough potatoes to eat. The teacher orders that he be served another spoonful but, once refilled, when the boy starts eating again, he overturns his plate and all the food falls to the floor. He cries even more than before.

Pini goes back home, puts away her books and goes to play in the field. At home her little niece keeps moaning. Pini's sister-in-law cannot cut vegetables peacefully. She goes to the fields and calls Pini back. Pini returns from playing in the field and organises other games with her little niece in front of the house.[69]

What happened when the performances took place in Calcutta, where nobody understood a word of Santhali (considered, in town, a 'dialect' even though it's a language in its own right)? The meaning remained deferred. During the first twelve minutes, Pini was talking heartily, suddenly pausing to sing or dance, quench her thirst, eat a cookie, approach the spectators, whisper something in someone's ear, stroke the hand of another, etc. During those first twelve minutes, the audience heard the text in Santhali, the sound of it, but did not have access to the translation.

If the subtitles had been shown from the start, the effect would have been quite distinct; it would have simplified and partly erased

---

[69] *Bachchader Experimentum* (2015–2016): https://trimukhiplatform.org/bachchader experimentum and https://youtu.be/0N3ALI58MsU (19:50).

what is only comprehensible through intimacy and experience.[70] Reading in English about a little Santhal girl's daily routine is much more *significant* after one has been lulled by the sound of her voice, gazed at her face for a long time (doubled on the wall behind, where her image, filmed live, was projected), taken pleasure in her movements, her approaches, withdrawals and glances. The experience is then more *meaningful* in the sense that this experience is now deeper: the depth of it being a consequence of the twelve-minute delay in the subtitle's appearance. The time spent not understanding gave time to dig into the present, to make the moment more relevant and more personal. As proof, here is what a spectator (Payal Trivedi) wrote to me after the performance:

> When the English subtitles appear facilitating the process of understanding Pini's speech, it certainly gives a direction in which to speculate. Primarily, I deconstruct the stereotyped understanding of the girl performing on the stage and interpret Pini's attempt as a carefree, playful, innocent gesture of enjoying and entertaining together which grabs our attention and gathers our admiration. When the subtitles appear, they certainly give me a route and I start construing the fact that it is Pini's story about her sister-in-law and the school boy who cries for curry. Now, at the basic level, understanding her language undeniably does give me the literal sense of what is being spoken which is important but it together opens up a possibility to interpret it in my own way, it becomes another avenue of exploration. As we begin understanding that Pini is talking about herself we wish to interpret in a different light based on what she speaks but without adamantly adhering to her words and the dictionary meanings they bear. In its use of tribal idiom and English subtitles, *Bachchader Experimentum* admirably gives us an interesting paradox. It provides the opportunity to dispense with the mandate of understanding language literally. Simultaneously, it also attests the need of language for generating

---

[70] Thai film-maker Apitchatpong Weerasethakul explained: 'It's a good thing not to understand; a good thing to be content enjoying a place, a moment, and synchronising with it to enjoy it' (*Libération*, 17 November 2021).

the possibility of newer meanings. In both cases, logocentrism is undermined.[71]

For the possibilities offered by a delay in understanding, we often have recourse to such a strategy. In *At the Beginning of Spring War Was Over*, the text is first spoken by an actor in English, then, shortly after and only partially, by another in Santhali and, finally, more than twenty minutes later, by an actress in Bengali.[72] Giving duration to *incomprehension*, it's giving depth to *apprehending*—the last term coming from late Latin *apprehendere* which translates as 'to seize, to grasp'. The duration causes changes in the nature of what was initially considered.

GRADATIONS IN INCOMPREHENSION

Following me until now, you have realised that I am proposing a kind of amusing gradation:

—first, an *announcement-text* that everyone can understand at first sight but that creates expectations which can then be thwarted in order to keep open (even catalysed) the attention and enlarge its spectrum;

—second, a *question-text* that everybody can understand but which, for its strangeness, is not plainly understandable, so inviting thinking and questioning oneself in a more personal manner;

—third, a densified thought text or *words wall* which, the reasoning it expounds being curled in on itself without producing the sensation of rejection, warmly invites us to go and think elsewhere;

—fourth, a combination of a *differences-accentuator-text* and a *relation-text* which must be understandable only for a part of the spectators so as to enhance (throughout troubling) the differences

---

[71] Extract of the testimony-analysis that Payal Trivedi sent to me by e-mail on 24 January 2016.
[72] *At the Beginning of Spring War Was Over* (2020): https://trimukhiplatform.org/atthebeginningofspringwarwasover and https://youtu.be/QFza22qlomo (English: 4: 05; Santhali: 6:22; Bengali: 30:31).

among the audience and invite (by redoubling the troubling) the weaving of relationships between these co-present differences;

—and fifth, a *delaying-text* whose dynamic of enunciation delays the moment of 'logical' comprehension and, by doing so, invites each spectator to deepen and enrich the experience lived meanwhile in the present moment.

Put end to end, these tropisms form a spectrum of possibilities, a polarised *continuum* of ways to play with literature. And, this is a point that I haven't detailed, mixed forms abound. Imagine, for instance, a *question-text* that is also a *delaying* one.

UNDERSTANDING THAT THERE IS NO NEED TO UNDERSTAND

Let's go a few steps further. Do interrupt your reading again to watch— and, of course, to listen to the following video extract: https://youtu.be/Z3qqCtrwjjk, starting at the sixth minute and fifty-third second.[73]

This is the last sequence of *Bachchader Experimentum* during one of the presentations in Calcutta. Four young people are perched on a tree. Continuously addressing the audience, they converse in Santhali, quietly at the beginning and almost shouting towards the end. Here is a text which does not meet any expectations regarding comprehension. On the contrary. Composed during rehearsals by the four actors (Joba, Ramjit, Surojmoni and Sukul Hansda) from indications I had given them, this words series was helping city spectators to *understand that there was nothing to understand*, at least nothing imposed from the start regarding meaning. The sentences and the gradually increasing volume of voices were modifying the quality of the audience attention. As a kind of insistent invitation whose insistent character was increasing.

In Spanish, you have the verb '*presenciar*' and the substantive '*presentificación*'. Perhaps we *presenciate* better, perhaps we appreciate more the presence of both what is there and what is coming, perhaps we are more attentive to what is presented and

---

[73] Direct access: https://youtu.be/Z3qqCtrwjjk&t=410.

what is about to arise in the present, when the words we listen to seem at first glance to say nothing to us. Because, in a way, what they then say to us is: '*you don't have to understand anything*' if you want to appreciate the presences with which these words compose. And then: '*if you understood us, or if you spent your time wondering what we supposedly wanted to convey, you would immediately stop listening to us and we would no longer move you.*' But when it works as on top of the tree, the series of words helps to prevent the spectators from settling in a situation of communication, immobilising themselves for the rest of the performance in a lackadaisical intellectual operation that they would be repeating in a loop.

Words are incentives to stop thinking of indifference to meaning as the loss of something. The lack is no longer a lack: it is a space to inhabit, a place to forge relationships in a different way. Payal Trivedi observed:

> My incapability of comprehending the [Santhali] language saves me the predicament of applying obstinate meanings to words which is a habit of logocentric sign for thing signified, which we humans are subject to.[74]

It is what philosopher Jean-Luc Nancy and choreographer Mathilde Monnier called 'the stake of *non-significance*'.[75] If texts help in this task, it is precisely because they are made with words—words being what one is supposed to first be 'applying obstinate meanings' to. When words invite us to consider their successions as *a-signifying*,[76] they become energetic tools to ensure practically a deepening and a widening of the experience that one has while listening to them. Their efficiency is libidinal: they sharpen the spectators' senses, set them in motion, in inner movements.[77]

(Of course, if we were, for example, watching a gathering of baboons 'talking' to us, we would expect not to understand, and,

---

[74] Another extract taken from Payal Trivedi's testimony-analysis.

[75] Jean-Luc Nancy, Mathilde Monnier, *Allitérations: Conversations sur la danse* (Paris: Galilée, 2005), p. 34.

[76] Cf. Jean-Luc Nancy, *Corpus* (Paris: Métailié, 2000), p. 23.

[77] Cf. Jean-François Lyotard, *Économie libidinale* (Paris: Minuit, 1974), pp. 306–307.

therefore, there would be no necessity for a shift in our inner presumptions.[78])

STRONG OR WEAK

And we can be more specific. The tree text participates in a process of intensification. The audience has neither time nor space to rest. Everyone is flung forward and constantly obliged to proceed, continuously pushed ahead. Driven by the flow of words spoken in a foreign language, no one has the possibility to halt and focus on their meaning. It is a question of a rhythm that the multiplication of voices accentuates and fortifies. Here, the combination of words forms what I call a *strong-text*. It's the strategy of the host who hits on the shoulder his guest and, making him or her lose balance, forces him or her to move forward and rush inside.

Or well, the process will participate in a sort of weakness, this time as a benevolent host would do for his guest at the threshold of his home: withdrawing to allow the spectator-guest to enter at his or her whim, letting him or her wander as he or she pleases. It's the seat left vacant at the table in Poland, as well as according to nomadic hospitality customs. In this *weak-text*, there is neither fullness nor force but silences, gaps, breaks and breaches. Their function is to manage empty spaces inside the flow of words to make it easier for the listener to enter and start inhabiting the area. Here is an example:

> [*Records played as four dancers fall, get up, fall again while a fifth one leans on a tree.*] Als dit de aarde is zou ik het anders noemen. Niet dat er iets mis mee is. Het is enigszins beschimmeld. Er zitten rauwe randjes aan. Niet dat dat ook erg is. Maar ergens heeft het iets vies. Het borrelt en bruist. Alsof er geen begin en einde is. Maar ergens in het midden. Zag ik dat het anders kon zijn. In den beginne was de aarde. Een wereld die borrelde en bruiste van energie. Maar misschien was het ook wel een wereld van regenwormen. Die zich door het duister drongen. En langzaam gaatjes prikten in het heelal. Alles daartussen zou je kunnen noemen een vorm van zijn.

---

[78] This last observation is the fruit of a conversation with Anjum Katyal.

Een vorm van zijn die nog geen vorm mag hebben. Zachtjes alsof god niet bestond. En alles godvergeten verlaten was.[79]

No need to say: for this text to bear all its fruits, for its moving and inspiring powers to be properly exercised, it is necessary that you do not understand anything of the Dutch language ...

DIVERSIFYING EXPERIENCES

... And even if this condition is fulfilled, it is likely that you do not see yet why this text would be a *weak* one, participating in a sort of recess, withdrawal and welcoming gap. There are two reasons. First reason: reading written sentences or listening to them spoken are different activities that call for different attention spans. If, when we were preparing *At the Beginning of Spring*, this series of words seemed to come very aptly, it was when all of us heard it pronounced by visual artist Ruchama Noorda—who had composed it—and not while reading it. Especially since, like those authored by Kajol Hansda or the actors in the tree, this series was composed orally, that is, without going through a written process.

Listen to it now: https://youtu.be/QFza22qlomo (starting at the fifteenth minute, thirtieth second).[80]

The excerpt will have enabled you to infer it: the operating mode of such a words series is similar to that of a *weak-text* for this second reason that it is part of an arrangement in which are inscribed dancers in movement, trees, insects, bird sounds, etc. Taken on its own, the series does not have these effects. And this observation applies to all the literary texts we studied. The series that begins with '*If you would be me and I would be you*' was not producing the same effects when the actress who was saying it (Émilie Leconte, in France in the second half of the 1990s) performed a score of movements while a video projection showed her in rehearsal or when another who was also saying it (Dulce Sanchéz, in Mexico in the mid-2000s) was almost motionless in the semi-darkness, holding at arm's length

---
[79] Text composed and recorded by Ruchama Noorda.
[80] Direct access: https://youtu.be/QFza22qlomo&t=930.

a lighted light bulb. The modus operandi was different if the phrase, pronounced later by the same actresses (in French and in Bengali), was part of a purely sound artwork; and different if part of a film: compare the *Poetry track* elaborated for our series *#HomemadeJoy* by Rogelio Sosa (https://soundcloud.com/trimukhiplatform/poetrytrack7) with the *Video-poem* I subsequently edited (https://youtu.be/Q5MvzF028II). Since the artwork including the *same* text is not the *same*, the text has *different* effects depending on the different arrangements it is part of.

More generally, calculating the effects produced by a literary text is a completely utopian operation: it is *u-topos*, etymologically *with no place* where to take place. It is an assumption with no real area of application. It is, however, a necessary hypothesis since it is a strategic one. Of course, it would seem quite absurd to qualify as a *strong text* the series of sentences pronounced from the tree while a spectator (Payal Trivedi) insists on the 'feeling of ethereal bliss' she experienced, details the expansion within her of a 'joy that art of dance brings' and describes the 'ecstasy' that it entails. Having an airy and ecstatic feeling has nothing to do with experiencing the density of a strong push. No matter: it is not that my hypothesis could have been false, it is that the place where what takes place finally does take place is the heart of a specific spectator. And this is an area the exact coordinates of which, as a director, I will never have. But the hypothesis, however u-topical it may be, is for me necessary since it allows me to glimpse the diversity of what would eventually arise for others while we compose with words. Naming this kind of text precisely in this specific composition helps to differentiate it from another kind in another composition. By saying this (*strong-text*) is different from that (*weak-text*), we are already conceiving of two sorts of series. Then to say this one is distinct from that other one (*announcing-text*) is to count a third one. The names I give to these series are tools at my disposal to diversify diversity. Naming differences is a way of opening the range of possibilities.

And I am not alone: during rehearsals, we are several 'others' operating together. This is how diversity becomes unpredictable, huge and even incommensurable.

DECENTERING

The texts we use in our dance-theatre performances, sound art pieces and video installations displace, question, delay and sometimes cancel out the possibility of logical understanding. They force the odyssey of senses to deepen and sense (i.e. meaning) to be fabricated differently, in a more singular and deeper way. In this, our literary texts decentre each spectator. They work to broaden his or her own experiences, opening possibilities for these experiences to occur elsewhere than in such or such centre that one would have believed to be the main and only one.

These texts are texts *for* theatre (or *for* film-theatre, screen dance, etc). They are fabricated before or during rehearsals. But there are also texts fabricated after the performance has happened. Payal Trivedi's is one of these. Here is another one written by tale-teller Marie-Laurence Chevallier after watching *My Body Is Another Landscape*:

> Crossing of bodies in water, on water, on earth, in trees, around trees, in the landscape. Body as an integral part of nature, in one direction or another. Crossing water with animals. Like a mandatory passage or the animal carried or washed as a child. The woman who puts on and off her sunglasses. What glasses to wear? The older couple who show us how to watch. Are they a threshold of what we are going to see? Movement of water, in water, of nature, bodies that appear, disappear. The movement of a young girl's hand towards the sky. The boy who does the same. A face projected on a tree trunk. A tree that has become a mirror of another ourselves. And then, an everyday element: the stool, to sit on and ... the gestures of the boys who caress their own face and rise to the sky. The top of the sky and the bottom of the earth, feet, on and under water. Movements, displacements and absence of movement, observation, gaze. Lying down, standing. I have myself too made a crossing. I'm not sure which one, but it was a beautiful crossing.[81]

---

[81] Written testimony received by e-mail on 13 December 2020.

Marie-Laurence's writing was about a page long while Payal Trivedi's totalled 3,814 words. Each of them decentres the very idea of 'literary text'. They are not texts *for* theatre but texts *from* theatre, not being written *before* the performance but *after*, not *deconstructing* the comprehension but *constructing* another one, not *questioning* but *answering*, bringing meaning in a personal way by making sense out of an aesthetic experience.

Payal and Marie-Laurence are in the same situation as Marcel Proust who, at the end of *In Search of Lost Time*, because a spoon hits a plate, feels 'the joy of the real found again' and decides to start writing. Proust decides to compose a long series of words because 'it was necessary to try to interpret the sensations, to try to think, that is to say, to draw out from the penumbra what [he] had felt, and to convert it into a spiritual equivalent' and to share it.[82] And nobody will deny that what Marcel Proust wrote, *In Search of Lost Time*, is an eminently literary text.

So, let's insist: there is a literary text that is not the starting point of a theatre or a video-dance show but its point of arrival. Not at first but at last. Not the cause but the consequence. Not literature becoming theatre or film but film or theatre becoming literature. That is to say: the place where literature is fabricated is also decentred.

But extending the scope of literature does not mean going back to the idea that everything would be in one way or another a 'text' (or a 'textuality') and that all lively experiences should be understood as a 'language' that semioticians would dissect.[83] No way: in the arrangement in which it is taken, the text is not everything, it is one specific element, and often it is nothing. For instance, when whatever of importance is happening doesn't depend on words: one of the texts from *My Body Is Another Landscape* has no effect at all on Marie-Laurence's experience, not even a musical one.

---

[82] Marcel Proust, *Le Temps retrouvé* (Paris: Gallimard, 'Folio', 1990), pp. 186, 185.
[83] The date of death of the semiotic is September 1972, during the lecture 'The tooth, the palm' that Jean-François Lyotard gave in Venice to semioticians.

MULTIPLYING THE AUTHORS
IN ORDER TO MULTIPLY THE 'WITH'

Decentring the place where literature is fabricated also means multiplying its 'authors'. Because who is the 'writer' now? Who are the 'composers' of these 'literary' lines? A rural farmer (Kajol Hansda), a city-dweller (Indrani Mallick) or a Nobel Prize for Literature winner (Peter Handke)? A French director over-graduated (me) or a very poorly educated Santhal girl (Pini Soren)? An art critic from the 'traditional high castes' (Payal Trivedi), a philosopher coming from an 'average' middle class (Gilles Deleuze) or members of 'scheduled tribes' (Ramjit, Sukul, Surojmoni Hansda)? The answer is: all of them, all of us. Because without this diversity of people, these sentences series would not have come to life. Without Pini, Surojmoni, Joba, Sukul and Ramjit's phrases, no text by Payal would have been written. Without the Santhal youth's wording, the Indian lady would not have felt the desire to compose one.

The game applies within our own artistic team. During *Ḥésèd*, a performance we rehearsed and presented in France, a text was heard by the audience, at the beginning in French, then in Santhali and, towards the end, in Bengali.[84] We had an intense writing process in three stages (Gilbert Simondon would have spoken of a *transductive* operation from one mother tongue to another to another).[85] First, I collected poems that I had recently written, selected parts, rearranged phrases and inserted new ones, playing with grammatical incorrectness and deliberately including words that did not exist in French. Secondly, Sukla Bar made a Bengali version of my twenty-five lines with neologisms and non-proper expressions as well. Her text was different from mine: in a way, it was another poem. Third, Sukul Hansda translated and recomposed most of her phrasing so the sentences flowed and the vocabulary variations operated in a troubling but appealing way in Santhali too. It took him more than a week and several glasses of wine.

---

[84] *Ḥésèd* (2023): https://trimukhiplatform.org/hesed.
[85] About the concept of 'transduction', see Gilbert Simondon, *L'individuation à la lumière des notions de forme et d'information* (Grenoble: J. Millon, 2005), p. 32.

Being a literary composer does not position one as hanging above the others (above the 'rest' of the public, let's say) but as irremediably immersed among them. Becoming an 'author' means playing the weaving relationships game more and more. It is not a sign of election but a proof of oddity. It is accepting the imperative of abnormality, of constant changes. In the same way, there is no general and permanent typology for characterising literary compositions, there are no standards in literature. And there are no *a priori* rules to compose with diversity.

Increasingly, from North and South America, Western and Eastern Europe, from Africa and from Asia, we are told that racism is *a must* and that making money is *the best*. That's why my locally circumscribed literary typology is far less innocent than it appears to be. Its dynamic consists in proposing to work with warmly meaningful nonsenses, nonsenses radically different from the double meaninglessness ruling our *marketed* and *right-winged* societies.[86]

And here is a why to fabricating literary texts as we do in Borotalpada tribal village: to give the desire to others to write other texts. That is to say, yes, to extend the field of literature, not as an invasion but as a space for sharing, and sharing something other, other even than literature itself: a sense of agency. If only this one: the joy, more than compelling today, of gathering and weaving together.

---

[86] On the one hand, 'young people in Europe and North America in particular, but increasingly throughout the world, are being psychologically prepared for useless jobs, trained in how to pretend to work, and then by various means shepherded into jobs that almost nobody really believes serve any meaningful purpose. Economies around the world have, increasingly, become vast engines for producing nonsense'. David Graeber, *Bullshit Jobs: A Theory* (London: Penguin, 2018, pp. 143, 146). On the other hand, racism 'is an imaginary structure that escapes the limitation of the concrete reality, of the senses. For a racist person, to see a "Nigger", it's not to see that he is not here; that he doesn't exist; that he is only the pathological fixation point of a lack of relationship'. (Achille Mbembe, *Critique de la raison nègre*, Paris: La Découverte, 'Poche', 2015, pp. 57, 58.) Assigning someone a racial identity is only possible if you don't really look at him or her or look at him or her without seeing him or her. It's to be blind to reality. In this *sense*, it is also *nonsense*.

Beyond the Tangible

Gurvinder Singh

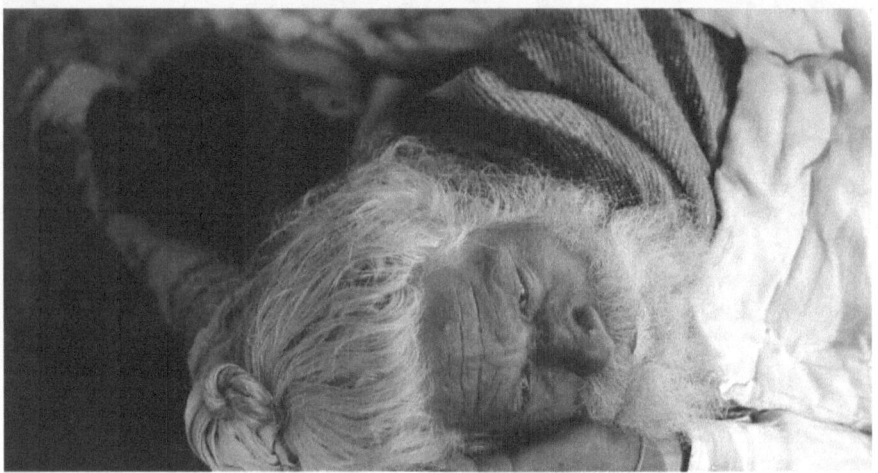

These images are from the prologue of *Anhey Ghorey Da Daan*, or Alms For the Blind Horse, a film dealing with the angst, alienation and exploitation of the marginalised castes in the Punjab that I made in 2011. Based on the novel of the same name by the celebrated Punjabi writer Gurdial Singh. When I completed the film and shared it with a prestigious international film festival, the director of the festival very enthusiastically had it included in the programme. I could not have asked for more for my debut feature. But my joy at having been selected for this elite festival was shortlived, as within a few days I received a 'list' of suggestive cuts and changes, which though not obligatory on my part to implement, I was nevertheless asked to seriously consider for the 'betterment' of the film. And a major part of this suggested overhaul of the film included getting rid of this prologue which ran for about nine minutes, leading to the opening credits. The programmer argued that it does not in any way impact the story of the film. That the story could very well begin post this sequence of 'family waking up' in the twilight hour and going about their mundane daily routine: daughter struggling to light the firewood wet with dew; father lying listless in the courtyard after waking up; mother too tired to wake up early; son too lazy to take the goats for grazing. Perhaps the programmer felt these 'events', if one could call them so, were not worthy of the soon-to-unravel conflict, and it was better to get directly into the meat of things than create a framework to receive them. An argument not dismissible in its entirety, if the only purpose of cinematic narrative was to posit cause and effects, conflicts and resolutions or a cycle of those. But is that the only reason films are made and viewed? What would be lost if I were to remove this entire segment from the film? What would the film gain other than reduced time length, if that was a welcome gain in the first place? For me it was very clear that the film would become experientially poorer. It might not be effected spatially or thematically, but the quality of experience and attention would undergo an unwelcome change. And if the film underwent an experiential change, whose film would it be?

According to Henri Bergson, the whole is not given or giveable, because according to him it is 'open', because its nature is to endure constantly, or to give rise to something new, in short, to endure. Each time we find ourselves confronted with a duration, or in a duration, we may conclude that there exists somewhere a whole which is changing, and which is open somewhere. Was the curator looking for a quick closure and did not have the necessary quality of attention to endure, or was she acting and forewarning me on behalf of an audience she perceived to lack this quality? Perhaps.

I stuck to my guns and refused to oblige the festival curator. Though the festival did screen the film, I was given a cold shoulder at the event, even being informed that my refusal to comply with the suggested cuts finished my chances of winning any award. Welcome to the world of curatorship, I said! But such instances only steel your resolve and make you even more stubborn to inflict the misery of 'time' and 'attention' on your audience.

Attention or *dhyaan*: an idea I first came across sitting in a classroom with my teacher Mani Kaul. Till then the word only conveyed an idea of command and discipline, forever having been told in school to pay attention. I wondered what it had to do with cinema.

Having been taught in film school that film thrives on privileged instants, on the Eisensteinian model of movements or developments extracted from moments of crisis, on collision of ideas and thematic reasoning, enduring or attending to information, however rarefied or saturated and unfolding in time, was perhaps what had escaped all of us. It completely changed my way of looking at cinema, of looking through the camera. From an obsession with space and information, I started seeking out duration, time and attention. The film turned from a visual art into a delightful temporal form. From information juxtaposed from one set to another set, it turned into a juxtaposition of attentions and durations, of tonalities and temporal volumes.

It rid me of the notion that cinema was a visual art. The visual was easy to grasp and create and replenish. The way of seeing, the angle of seeing, the character of light on objects and faces and bodies, the arrangement of objects, the graphic quality of the image were all in the domain of the visible. It was the material of cinematic image, concrete and tangible, that constituted narration in conjunction with a relay of words. But without knowing, the obsession with the image had become a hindrance. Was it merely information that one was chasing? How could an image turn from carrier of information into a carrier of feelings?

I got back to my own experiences of reading literature, listening to music and watching films. The films that had me hooked were films which I could not grasp, the films in which I was not even mentally present in the world of the story unfolding on the screen. The best films were the ones which took me 'elsewhere'. Or reading *One Hundred Years of Solitutde* without even bothering to know about the 'xyz' of the story and its plot points. Just going on reading because it was a thrill to read, because the words were a delight to confront, because the descriptions were leading to vivid imaginations of spaces and textures and smells and sounds and faces and colours. The writing was leaving impressions which one need not decode but which left one with a sense of curiosity about the external and internal world. If someone asked me what the story was, I could not say even a sentence about it. At least, that is my memory of it now. Or maybe I could at that time.

Bergson in the first chapter of *Matter and Memory* theorises: there are not only instantaneous images or movement images; there are finally time-images, that is, duration-images, change-images, relation-images, volume-images which are beyond movement itself.

That which is beyond movement has to be beyond the spatial, beyond the visible and graspable. Can duration itself be that image? If evocation of feelings is the ultimate goal of cinematic storytelling, then perhaps yes, duration can be that carrier. The resonance of an image of a tree unfolding in time will undergo drastic changes in perception, first, of course, in relationship to the set of images it is juxtaposed with, but more significantly with the time volume it occupies in the unfolding set of durations. The immediate feeling will be decoded from the angle and distance of view, the magnification of its physicality, the quality of light falling on the tree and its surroundings, and whether there is movement of objects impacting its presence, or whether the camera itself is mobile or immobile. This decoding is directly linked to the essential time required for this information to register. Let's say there is an objective idea of this time duration. The Hollywood director or the editor will say, 'Cut. That's it. I need not show it longer. It has done its job. Let's move on to the next set.' But perhaps someone else will come along and say: I am totally immersed in it and would want to stay immersed a little longer. Please let me pay attention for a longer stretch of time. It is evoking many things for me which I cannot describe. I am immersed in the experience it is creating for me. Or just the opposite, someone else would say: I don't want the feeling to register completely. It should be just like a whiff of smell which came and vanished, leaving you wondering where it came from and where it disappeared. But it has carried your senses along or even distracted them. It has provoked your sensibility to wonder. Both, according to me, are valid means to feelings, one perhaps leaving you breathless, and the other perhaps leaving you restless. The 'objective' sense of duration is perhaps the most obvious, which kills your sensibility to wonder. Because that sense reduces every set of objects to possessing an identical and objective set of notions and associations for the viewer. It reduces the seen and the seer to an average sensibility of meaning and looking and grasping things. Cinema: seen as a series of object sets organised to create a series of qualities of attentions, each one having the possibility of being abruptly killed in an instant and reborn with a new condition. As Gilles Deleuze said, the further duration descends into the system like a spider, the more effectively it creates the 'out-of-field', and fulfils its other function which is that of introducing the transspatial and the spiritual into the system which is never perfectly closed or decoded. Robert Bresson made this into an ascetic mode. The more his image is closed, even reduced to two dimensions, the greater is its capacity to open itself on to a fourth dimension which is time, and onto the fifth, which Deleuze calls the 'Spirit'.

To quote Bresson: 'If an image, looked at by itself, expresses something sharply, if it involves an interpretation, it will not be transformed on contact with other images. The other images will have no power over it, and it will have no power over the other images. Neither action, nor reaction. It is definitive and unusable in the cinematographer's system.'

'Apply myself to insignificant (non-significant) images.'

What is this non-significant and what is its importance in the scheme of storytelling, especially for the filmmaker? Our lives don't comprise of significant instants every moment of our breathing. So why should a work of art aspire to that unrealistic objective? To create is to tie new relationships between persons and things. And extended to film, it involves tying new relationships between time itself which can give rise to new feelings. And as Bresson said: 'Let it be the feelings that bring about the events. Not the other way.'

Notes on the Contributors

Tiffany Atkinson is a poet and critic based in Norwich, UK. Her most recent poetry collection, *Lumen* (Bloodaxe 2021) was a Poetry Book Society Recommendation and winner of The Medicine Unboxed Creative Prize. She received the Cholmondeley Award for Poetry in 2022. She is currently working on a fifth poetry collection, and completing a monograph entitled *O What Can I Say: Poetry, Ethics and Embarrassment*, for which she received a Leverhulme Research Fellowship. She is Professor of Creative Writing (Poetry) at the University of East Anglia.

Charles Bernstein is the author or editor of over 50 books, ranging from collections of poetry and essays to pamphlets, libretti, and collaborations, most recently *Topsy-Turvy* (2021) and *Pitch of Poetry* (2016), both from the University of Chicago Press. Bernstein co-directs of PennSound and is Donald T. Regan Professor, Emeritus, of English and Comparative Literature at the University of Pennsylvania. He is the winner of the 2019 Bollingen Prize from Yale for lifetime achievement in poetry and a Fellow of the American Academy of Arts & Sciences.

Amit Chaudhuri edits Literary Activism.

Jeremy Harding is a British writer and journalist based in France. He is a contributing editor at the *London Review of Books*. His books include *Border Vigils: Keeping Migrants Out of the Rich World* and *Mother Country*, a memoir.

Arvind Krishna Mehrotra is a poet, translator, and editor of several anthologies. He lives in Dehradun.

Geoffrey O'Brien is the author of twelve prose books, including *Where Did Poetry Come From* (2020) and *Arabian Nights of 1934* (2023), and ten collections of poetry, most recently *Who Goes There* (2020) and *Went Like It Came* (2023). His essays on film, poetry, opera, and other subjects have appeared frequently in *The New York Review of Books*, *Artforum*, *Film Comment*, *The Village Voice*, and other periodicals. He was an editor at The Library of America for 25 years, retiring as editor-in-chief in 2018.

Anjum Hasan's latest novel is *History's Angel*. She is the author of *A Day in the Life*, *The Cosmopolitans*, *Neti, Neti, Lunatic in my Head*, *Difficult Pleasures*, and *Street on the Hill*.

Jean-Frédéric Chevallier is a philosopher, dance-theatre director, and video artist. A lecturer at the Sorbonne Nouvelle University in Paris during his PhD studies and then a professor at the National University of Mexico for seven years, he radically changed course in 2008 by choosing to operate from a tribal village in India: a unique journey that opened up the possibility of practising the arts and thinking in a more contemporary and unpredictable way. In French, he has published the essays *Deleuze and the Theatre* (Les Solitaires Intempestifs, 2015) and *The Theatre of Presenting* (Circé, 2020) as well as the poetry collection *Then from the World Something Comes* (Trimukhi Platform, 2022).

Gurvinder Singh is an Indian film director. He is best known for his Punjabi language films *Anhe Ghore Da Daan* and *Chauthi Koot* (*The Fourth Direction*) which premiered at Venice and Cannes Film Festival respectively.

OTHER TITLES IN THE LITERARY ACTIVISM SERIES

Book of Rahim & Other Poems by Arvind Krishna Mehrotra

On Being Indian by Amit Chaudhari

Treasurer of Piggy Banks by Vinod Kumar Shukla, translated by Arvind Krishna Mehrotra

www.ingramcontent.com/pod-product-compliance
Lightning Source LLC
LaVergne TN
LVHW041604070526
838199LV00049B/2138